Macramé Jewellery

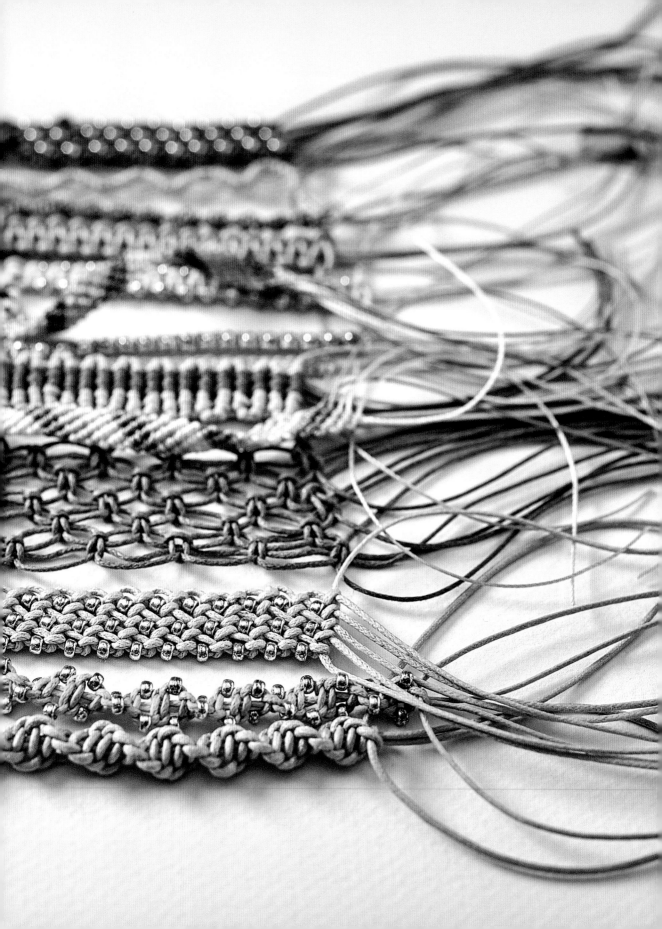

Macramé Jewellery

The visual guide to everything
you need to know

Jenny Townley
and Suzen Millodot

QUARTO PRESS

Macramé Jewellery
A QUARTO BOOK

First published in 2016 by
Quarto Press
The Old Brewery
6 Blundell Street
London N7 9BH
www.quartoknows.com

ISBN 978-0-85762-148-1

10 9 8 7 6 5 4 3 2 1

QUAR.MACJ

Senior Project Editor: Chelsea Edwards
Senior Art Editor and Designer: Jackie Palmer
Photographers: Nicki Dowey (location),
    Phil Wilkins (studio)
Design Assistant: Martina Calvio
Copy Editor: Caroline West
Proofreader: Claire Waite Brown
Indexer: Helen Snaith
Art Director: Caroline Guest
Creative Director: Moira Clinch
Publisher: Paul Carslake
Colour separation by PICA Digital Pte Ltd,
    Singapore
Printed by 1010 Printing International Ltd,
    China

FSC
www.fsc.org

MIX
Paper from
responsible sources
FSC® C016973

Quarto is the authority on a wide range of topics.

Quarto educates, entertains and enriches the lives of
our readers — enthusiasts and lovers of hands-on living.

www.quartoknows.com

Contents

I first discovered macramé as a child. I grew up during the hippy sixties, when friendship bracelets abounded. Making my own bracelets was my very first introduction to macramé, and really sparked my interest in the craft.

Later in life I started to make costume jewellery, and stumbled across some very beautiful and what looked like very intricate pieces of micro-macramé jewellery. Being a crafter, I wanted to know how to recreate this type of work for myself, so I bought many books, practised and taught myself. My first attempts were pretty dismal, but I kept on trying, correcting my errors as I developed, and now here I am writing my own books on the subject for others!

Macramé can be anything you want it to be, and that is what makes it special. From delicate friendship bracelets to chunky chevrons and lacy cuffs, you'll be sure to find something to suit your style. You choose the colours, the cords, the beads and the knots and the book will help you to make what you want.

Armed with this book and your imagination, the macramé world is your oyster.

Jenny Townley

I used to admire intricate Celtic knot designs and wonder if they had ever been made using actual cords. So when we went to live in Hong Kong and I 'discovered' Chinese knots, which were made with special satin cords in many beautiful shapes, designs and colours, I was determined to learn how to make them.

I began to make jewellery with Chinese knots and beads, in a more Western style than traditional Chinese knotted jewellery, and eventually wrote a book about the knots and their folklore, and projects on how to make them.

Upon discovering micro macramé I found it to be very versatile, the knots are simple yet it is possible to make very creative and attractive jewellery with them, as you can see from Jenny's lovely designs. I really enjoy the freedom that macramé gives us to create original pieces.

I have introduced some Chinese and Celtic knots that complement macramé well. The versatile Button Knot is great for hiding cord ends and finishing jewellery, and the Chinese Dew Knot is a different way of gathering cords together and also makes an attractive braid called a Snake Knot. The Double Coin Knot (aka Josephine Knot) is shown here created with a braid of Square Knots, and a Celtic Square Knot is made with a braid of Lark's Head Knots; perfect combinations of macramé and Chinese and Celtic knotting.

Suzen Millodot

About This Book

With its informative, colourful and step-by-step led approach, by using this book you will soon become an expert in all things macramé. For amateurs and practised individuals alike, this book begins by telling you what equipment you will need, the skills you will learn and the different materials you can use. Every aspect of the book has been designed with the reader in mind, from variations in knot usage, ideas on how to personalize your jewellery and video clips that guide you through trickier knots. The book ends with a selection of projects for you to create, and a handy fold-out flap to use as a reference while you work.

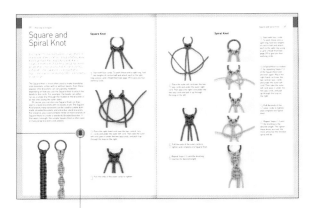

STEP-BY-STEP IMAGERY
Close-up images with step-by-step instructions of the knot allow you to see how your macramé pieces should look.

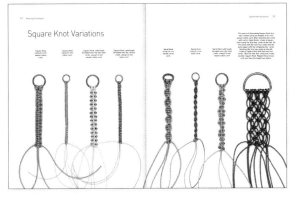

KNOT VARIATIONS
Variations on the type of knot you will be tying are displayed, clearly showing you the range of looks you can achieve.

VIDEO CLIPS
Where you see the phone icon we have put together a video to provide a visual reference to guide you through the knot formation. All of the QR codes which link to the videos are on page 96.

PROJECTS
Clear step-by-step photographs are accompanied by beautiful images of each finished jewellery piece, which will hopefully inspire you to have a try!

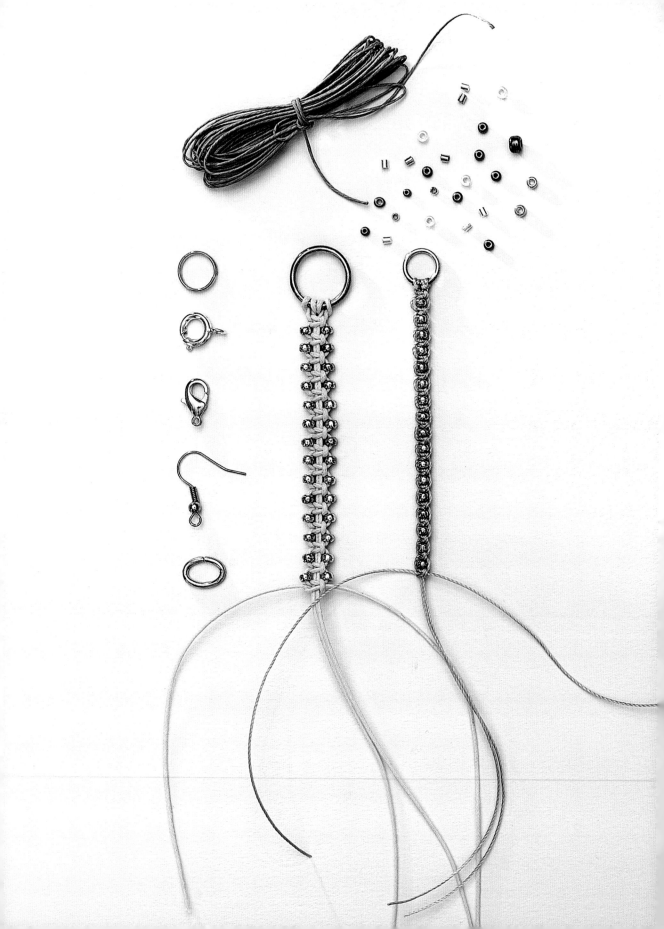

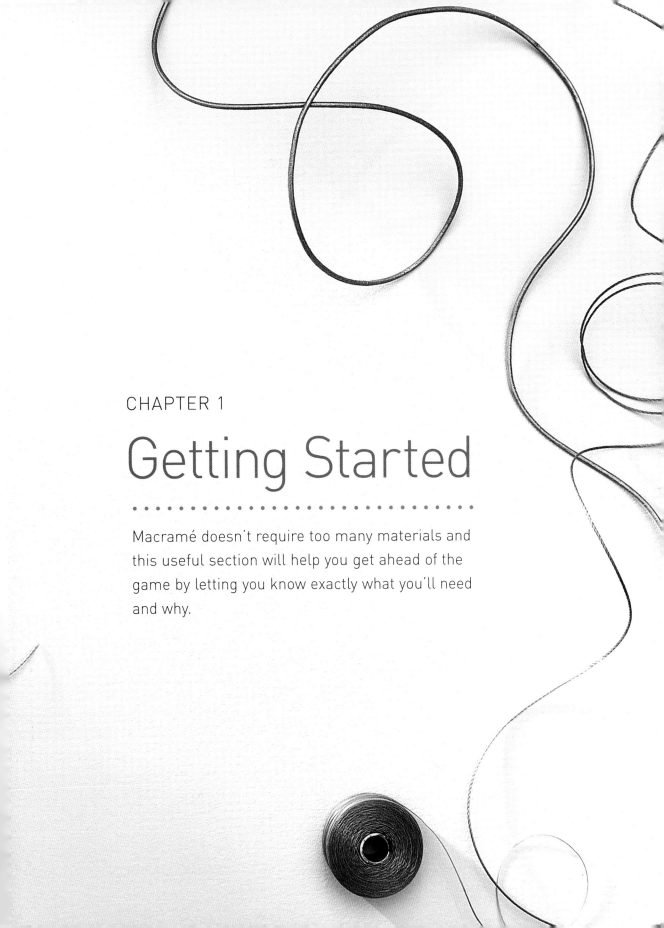

CHAPTER 1

Getting Started

· ·

Macramé doesn't require too many materials and
this useful section will help you get ahead of the
game by letting you know exactly what you'll need
and why.

Cords

We are fortunate to have an excitingly wide range of cords for knotting to choose from. There are cords of all types and thicknesses, making it easy to find the perfect one for each project.

The main types of macramé cords are C-Lon twisted nylon cords, Chinese knotting cords, satin cords, waxed cotton cords, Korean knotting cords, linen cords and leather cords.

C-Lon twisted nylon cords (1)

These cords are made from three-ply, twisted, nylon strands in two thicknesses: a standard 0.5 mm cord and a heavier C-Lon Tex 400, which is almost 1 mm thick. Both of these cords are available in over 100 colours, which is an artist's dream. They have a lovely sheen that makes your work look very attractive. The colours vary from subtle to bright jewel shades. C-Lon cords are excellent for simpler macramé knots that do not need much handling (i.e. the Square Knot and the alternating Half Hitch Knot). With more complicated

knots, the 'twist' can become untwisted and make your work look untidy. The Tex 400 is usually my cord of preference, but the final choice will also depend on the hole size of the beads you want to use.

Chinese knotting cords (2)

Like C-Lon cords, these are also made from nylon, but are braided. They are, therefore, sturdier cords that are ideal for micro-macramé knots and Chinese knotting. They can also hold a curve very well, because they have more 'body' than twisted cords. I prefer to use Chinese knotting cords for Snake Knots, Lark's Head Knots, Double Coin Knots and Celtic Square Knots because of their firmness and strength. They are available in various thicknesses, ranging from 0.4 mm to 2 mm.

The only disadvantage of these cords, compared with C-Lon twisted cords, is that there are far fewer colours to choose from and these can also vary from one dye lot to another.

Satin cords (3)

There are two types of satin cords (or rattail cords): nylon satin cords, which are mainly from China and Taiwan, and rayon satin cords that are made in the USA. It is easy to tell just by looking at the cords if they are made from nylon or rayon, since rayon is much more shiny.

Nylon satin cords are largely used for Chinese and Celtic knotting. Nylon cord is easier for beginners to use, since it holds a knot well, while rayon cord is more slippery and does not hold the knot as well.

Rayon cords have a cotton core, which has the advantage of not

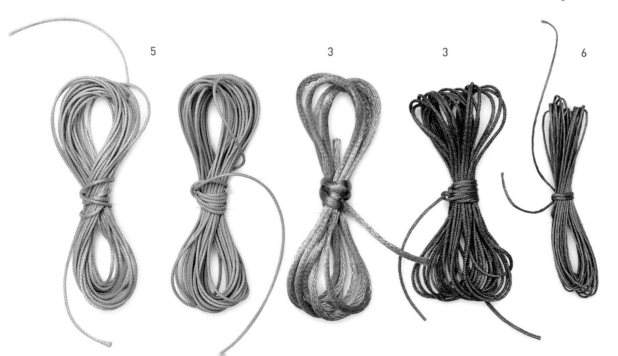

5   3   3   6

stretching after the knotting is finished. Your choice will depend on the effect you wish to achieve.

Satin cords come in various thicknesses, from 1 mm to 2 mm (and also 3 mm, although this isn't often used for making jewellery). The ends of nylon cords can be heat-sealed, unlike those of rayon cords.

Both types of cord are available in a wide range of colours. The nylon colours can be variable, but the rayon ones from the USA are much more reliable.

Cotton cords (4)

These cords are usually made from waxed cotton and are available in three different thicknesses: 1 mm, 1.5 mm and 2 mm. The cotton has more 'body' and the thicker ones are good for Chinese or Celtic 'stand-alone' knots, as the cord maintains a nice curve when used for knots such as the Double Coin Knot or the

Celtic Square Knot. However, it is not always easy to find the exact colour of cotton cord that you need.

Korean knotting cords (5)

These cords are excellent for knotting. They come in many different colours and thicknesses, from 1 mm to 2 mm. They have a cotton core with a braided rayon cover, which makes them fairly rigid and good for Chinese and Celtic knotting. However, as these are stiff cords, I find that they are not as comfortable for necklaces, where the knotted portion is in contact with the back of the neck; softer satin cords are more comfortable to wear. Korean knotting cords are not easily available in the UK, but can be purchased by mail order from the USA.

Linen cords (6)

These cords come in various thicknesses (between 0.7 mm and

1 mm), as well as a variety of colours, and are usually waxed. Linen cords tend to have more 'body and tooth' than cotton cords.

Leather cords (7)

These cords can be very beautiful. Nowadays they are of a good quality and are available in a wide range of colours and many thicknesses, from 0.5 mm to 3 mm.

They can be either flat or round. Leather cords are very good for 'stand-alone' knots with curved loops such as the Double Coin Knot or Celtic-style knots. However, they do not like to be pulled about in tighter knots, such as the Chinese Button Knot, which needs to be tightened, moved and handled a lot in general. Although leather cords come in many different colours, finding the exact colour you require for a particular project can be a slightly 'hit-or-miss' affair.

4   1   4   2

7

Beads and Buttons

When choosing beads or buttons for a project, the world is your oyster, as there are so many to choose from, not only in terms of design and colour, but also size.

10

Types of beads

Any shape of bead can be incorporated into macramé works and you are only limited by your imagination. If you're new to macramé, you may wish to begin with plain, round seed beads and then include more decorative beads as you become more experienced.

Seed beads (1)

Seed beads are shaped like a ring doughnut and are available in a wide range of sizes. However, sizes 11, 8 and 6 are probably the most popular for macramé work. The smaller the number, the larger the bead. You should always check the cords you are using against the size of the bead hole to make sure your choice will thread through the hole comfortably.

Cylinder beads (2)

'Cylinder bead' is a generic term used to describe beads that are shaped like a cut section of glass tubing with flat ends.

Bicone crystals (3)

Crystal beads come in various shapes and a multitude of colours and coatings. They fit together nicely and bring an element of bling to your work.

Pearls (4)

Pearls have long been a symbol of beauty and refinement, although the real thing can be quite expensive. However, you can now obtain 'fake' pearls on a crystal base, which combine quality with an affordable price. There is also an exciting range of colours to choose from.

Glass/lampwork beads (5)

There is a huge array of glass beads available, including striking pendants. Lampwork beads are handmade using rods of glass that are melted around a mandrel to create different shapes and textures. No two beads are alike and they are ideally suited to hand-knotted jewellery.

Ceramic beads (6)

Made from china or porcelain, some ceramic beads have big holes because they are either made on large rods or pierced with thick drills when the clay is still unfired.

Acrylic beads (7)

Acrylic or plastic beads are available in a wide range of colours, sizes and shapes, including objects such as flowers or stars. They also come in different textures and finishes. The opaque ones, for example, look attractive with coloured cord. They are often bought in large packs and are an economical option.

Shaped beads (8)

Feature beads come in many different shapes, including daggers, drops, cubes and discs. They can be used to add texture and interest to your work. When choosing them, pay close attention to where the holes lie.

Bead hole size

The most important factor to consider when you're choosing beads is the hole size. Since most cords are at least 1 mm thick, you need to ensure that the cord will fit through your choice of beads. There is little point buying beautiful beads that you are then unable to use because your cord is too thick to pass through the holes. Try a selection of beads with the cord you are planning to use, because not all beads have uniformly sized holes.

- 1 mm
- 1.5 mm
- 2 mm
- 2.5 mm
- 3 mm
- 3.5 mm
- 4 mm

Buttons (9)

Buttons make a great alternative to beads for creating a focal point in a macramé piece. However, you must ensure that the buttons either have a shank at the back or the holes at the front are large enough for threading your cords through.

Cabochons (10)

Cabochons are stones or glass cut with a flat bottom and a rounded top. They look lovely with bordered by macramé.

1

2

3

4

5

6

7

8

9

Findings

Findings are those little pieces of hardware that pull your macramé design together and transform it into an attractive and wearable piece. Here we look at some of the more common findings used in macramé.

Clasps

Clasps allow you to open or close your piece of macramé work when you are putting it on or taking it off. Often, the clasp you choose will be a matter of personal taste, but the most popular types are examined here.

Toggle clasp (1)

Toggle clasps consist of a bar and a ring. These types of clasps are very secure and easy to use, and are available in many different designs and sizes.

Lobster clasp (2)

A lobster clasp opens and closes by means of a spring-loaded trigger. Lobster clasps are slightly trickier to operate than other clasps, but are a very secure option.

Hook and S-hook (3)

A hook clasp usually consists of a hook and eye that link together, although sometimes they just come with the hook side. S-hooks are double-sided and shaped like an 'S'. These usually come with two rings. They are very easy to operate for most people. Both styles of hook clasp rely on the weight and fit of the piece to hold them in place.

Terminators

This is a blanket term used to describe the findings that finish off a piece of jewellery, either before the clasp or at a transition point (sometimes 'end clamps' is used instead of terminators). The three most commonly used are crimps, cord ends and ribbon ends.

Crimps (4)

Crimps are the most basic type of terminator. They are small metal tubes that are squeezed with pliers to hold the cords in place. Crimps may be round, square or rectangular in shape.

Cord ends (5)

Cord ends come in two basic styles: coil and fold-over. A coil cord end looks like a coil of wire with a ring at one end. The coil slides over the cord, and the last coil is squeezed tightly around the cord to secure it in place. A fold-over (or box) cord end is rectangular in shape, with two flaps that fold down over the cord to hold it inside.

Ribbon ends (6)

Ribbon ends are used for wide, flat connections to a single point, such as for wide cuff bracelets. The cords lie inside the ribbon end, and pliers are used to squeeze the ribbon end into place.

Jump rings (7)

Jump rings are metal rings that are open on one side. These findings are used to attach one piece to another – perhaps a clasp to a cord end. They come in many sizes to fit all types of projects and are measured by the diameter of the ring.

Earwires and posts (8)

Earwires are hook-shaped wires that slide through a pierced ear. Ear posts are straight pieces of wire that fit into pierced ears and are held in place with a butterfly at the back. Both earwires and ear posts are available with a small loop at the front from which you can suspend the main body of the earring.

Split rings and closed jump rings (9)

Split rings are double circles of metal, while closed jump rings are single circles of metal without the opening found on usual jump rings. These rings make an excellent choice to start off almost any project because the cord cannot slip out of the ring, as can happen with the opening in jump rings.

9

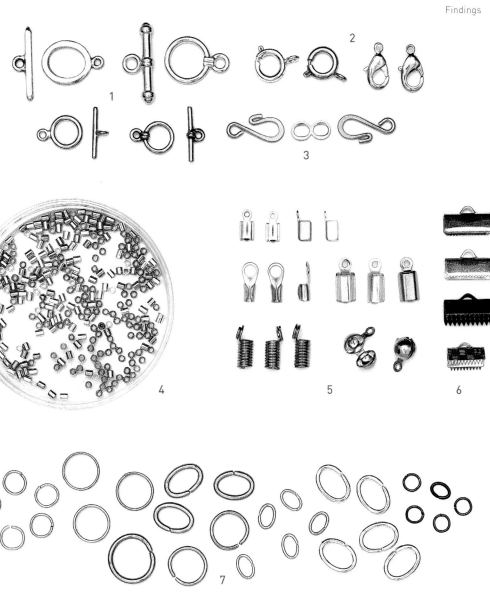

1

2

3

4

5

6

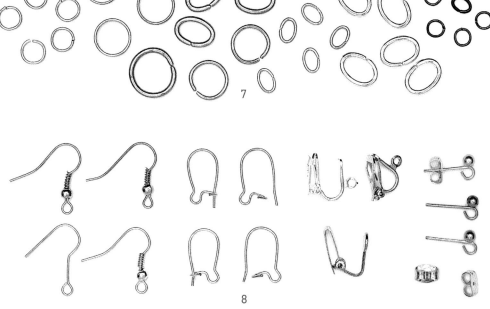

7

8

Tools

You do not need a great number of tools for successful macramé work, but there are a few items that will make your knotting much easier and more comfortable.

Macramé board (1)

You can use a cork placemat to anchor your knotting as you work, but a while ago a special foam macramé board became available. It is firm, takes repeated pinning and unpinning, and has notches along the sides that can hold some of the cords firmly while you knot (see pages 22–23).

Nail scissors (2)

It is recommended that you use very sharp scissors so the cords can be cut cleanly with no fraying. Fine nail scissors can be useful for finishing a project where the cord needs to be trimmed as close to the knot as possible.

Dressmaker's pins (3)

As this is micro macramé, which uses fine cords, it is important to use fine pins that will not spoil the cords. I find that dressmaker's pins work very well, and do not make your fingers sore. They are pleasant to handle and easy to find.

Tape measure or ruler (4)

Either of these tools will prove helpful when it comes to measuring out the length of the cords before you start work on your project.

Clear nail varnish (5)

If you intend to thread beads onto your cords, then the best way to do this by far is to brush clear nail varnish onto the ends of the cords to prepare them and then make a nice, stiff 'needle' end to help thread the beads. The stiff ends also help with some knots, because you can weave the cord in and out more easily without it curling up and evading your efforts. The most annoying part is waiting for the varnish to dry and become stiff. I usually try to prepare the ends the night before, but it is sometimes very difficult to be so organized!

Instant glue gel (6)

An alternative to PVA glue for sealing cord ends (see page 25), this glue is easy to use because it is a gel and makes a nice small drop just where you want it. Glue gel also comes in a special dispenser that you simply squeeze on the sides in order to dispense the glue. It is very useful for finishing off your macramé, as a small drop of instant glue on the end of the knotting can be trimmed when the glue is dry, either with a small pair of scissors or a special thread burner.

Thread burner (7)

This tool is optional and can only be used on synthetic cords. However, it seals and cuts the ends of the cords at the same time and leaves a neat finish. It is battery operated and much safer to use for sealing cord ends than a match or cigarette lighter (see page 25).

Pliers (8)

There is a huge variety of pliers on the market. You'll need to keep a small pair of needle-nose and flat-nose pliers to hand for attaching findings and opening and closing jump rings.

Thread cutter (9)

A thread cutter can be worn around the neck and helps keep sharp blades at a safe distance from your fingers.

Wax (10)

Coating thread with beeswax or silicone wax will help prevent unwanted knots. You'll also find that the thread will slip through your beads more easily.

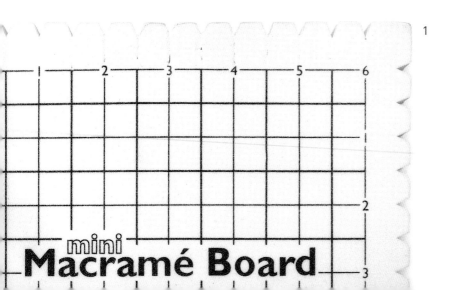

8

9

2

3

7

10

4

6

5

THREAD

Estimating Quantities

Estimating the quantities of cords and beads you'll need to make a macramé piece comes with practice, as is the case with most things. You'll learn to estimate accurately from experience, but here are a few rules-of-thumb to help you on your way.

When looking at various macramé or micro-macramé patterns, you may find yourself wondering why the amounts of cord needed appear to be a lot larger than you would think necessary. This could be down to a few different reasons:
• You need enough cord to create the item and the various knots will call for longer lengths of cord than the eventual length of the necklace, bracelet, earrings or whatever it is you're making.
• You need to make sure you have enough cord to work with. If you only have the exact amount, then you will find it very difficult to manipulate the cords as you wish.
• It can be very frustrating if you are close to finishing a piece only to discover that you are running short of cord and either have to abandon the project completely or find some way of attaching more cord so that you can finish off – this is not always an easy or tidy job to do. So, for these reasons, excess cord is often suggested in the majority of macramé patterns.

Cord widths

Cords come in many different widths, so you should bear this in mind before embarking on a project, especially if you are using beads, as you'll need to ensure the cord fits through the bead holes. Fine cords are well suited for making knotted jewelry – and will be the ones you use most for micro-macramé pieces – while thicker cords are perfect for making larger statement pieces

0.5 mm

1 mm

1.5 mm

2 mm

2.5 mm

3 mm

3.5 mm

4 mm

How long should my cord be?

When it comes to cords you can usually estimate the lengths required as follows:
Earrings = 61 cm (24 in)
Bracelets = 150 cm (60 in)
Necklaces = 380 cm (150 in)
The estimates given above are for those patterns that ask you to fold the cords in half when starting off your project, so that each cord becomes two working cords. If the pattern does not ask you to do this, then you will more than likely have to double these amounts. Please note that some knots also use much more cord length than others. For example, a Double Half Hitch Knot takes up more cord than a Square Knot. So, always allow yourself a little more cord when using this particular knot.

How many beads do I need?

It is difficult to estimate precisely how many beads you will need for a specific piece, but you will find that the smaller the size of the beads, the more of them you will need.

Bead (approximate size)	Beads per 2.5 cm (1 in)	Beads per 46 cm (18 in)	Beads per 61 cm (24 in)
Size 15 seed bead (1.5 mm)	17	307	401
Size 11 seed bead (1.8–2.2 mm)	12–14	210–256	278–339
Size 8 seed bead (3 mm)	8	140	185
Size 6 seed bead (4 mm)	6	115	153

The number of beads you require will vary radically depending on which pattern you choose, as well as the finished length of the piece. You'll also find that the size of seed beads varies according to the manufacturer, the finish on the bead and even the colour of the bead. However, the bead guide above provides a useful approximation of the average sizes and quantities, and may help when you start creating your own designs.

Bead sizes

The table below shows common bead sizes and gives an idea of the physical size of each and the number of beads per gram. The number representing the size of the bead indicates how many beads that will roughly fit in an inch when placed side by side.

Seed bead size	Approximate size	Number per 1 gram	Number per 10 grams	Number per 100 grams
Size 15	1.5 mm	250	2,500	25,000
Size 11	2.2 mm	120	1,200	12,000
Size 8	3 mm	36	360	3,600
Size 6	4 mm	18	180	1,800

Choosing Knots

Choosing knots is a question of texture and style, as well as personal preference. When designing a pattern, you'll need to work out which knots to use to create your masterpiece.

Button Knots

Diagonal Double
Half Hitch Knots

Match knots to patterns and cords

If you want to create an intricate pattern, then it is a good idea to stick with a knot you are comfortable with, as well as one that you can perform at its tidiest. This is because an intricate pattern will show up the tiniest of imperfections and irregularities in tension.

Knots can look very different depending on the types of cords you choose. It can be difficult, for example, to create a lacy cuff with a thick hemp cord. The effect would not be quite the same as if you were to use a much thinner nylon or soft, lightly waxed cotton cord.

You also need to decide whether you want to include beads with your knots.

The basic Square Knot is popular in a lot of designs and is always a safe knot to begin with. However, adding some beads can transform a plain macramé piece into something more elaborate and interesting. Incorporating some beads

with the alternating Square Knot, for example, would have quite a dramatic and sparkly effect. It would create a glitzy, lacy little bracelet. You can also create many different looks by adding different coloured beads to your knots.

The majority of **Chinese and Celtic knots** are knots that can stand alone, and need a thicker firmer cord than macramé knots require.

The Celtic Square Knot is very attractive and is ideal for making earrings as only one knot is needed to make a very unusual earring. **The Double Coin Knot** can stand alone or be made in a series, either side by side or one below the other. The Double Coin Knot knotted in a series with one below the other is perfect for bracelets, it is lacy and very pleasing and could also be pulled tighter to make a more solid knot.

Square Knots using beads on the
outer cords.

Celtic Square Knot

Square Knots
using beads on
the outer cords.

Series of Double Coin Knots

The Chinese Snake Knot is very versatile and makes a very sinuous braid that is great for bracelets and necklaces, it is a nice way to show off a special pendant and is more interesting than the usual metal chain as it can be made in a matching or contrasting colour. **The Dew Knot**, which is the basis of the Snake Knot, is also versatile and a single Dew Knot or one above the other is a good way of linking two pieces of cord.

The Button Knot is very versatile and its natural partner is 2 mm satin cords which looks very luxurious and goes beautifully with handmade lampwork beads. It can be made into a sliding knot and is very good as a finishing knot as the ends can be hidden within the knot to make a very elegant and tidy finish. It can be knotted with two cords as well, which is very useful when you want a 'statement' necklace or bracelet with more cords in different colours.

Combining different knots

You can give simple knots a whole new look and level of interest by combining them with other knots in a pattern. **The Overhand Knot** is often overlooked and generally only used to tie a few cords together in one simple step. However, it can be transformed into a very lacy pattern if it is made with several cords in a row. Row after row of **Diagonal Double Half Hitch Knots**, for example, would look completely different if they were broken up by several rows of alternating **Square Knots**. Try combining different knots in your patterns to create your own unique looks and designs. Just let your imagination loose – you may be pleasantly surprised at the results.

Snake Knot

Square Knots and Button Knots

Using a Macramé board

A macramé board will help keep your work neat and tidy but, most importantly, it will enable you to keep the tension consistent and to manage the cords you're working with.

Why pick a macramé board?

The macramé board has been specially designed for creating macramé and micro-macramé pieces. It is lightweight and easy to use, and ingeniously made with cut-out notches around the outside that are perfect for holding the cords in place. A macramé board has the added advantage of a grid marked out in inches and half-inches to help you estimate cord quantities. The board is also made from a material that is self-healing, which means that, in most cases, those annoying pin holes disappear after time. Specially designed, long-shanked pins can be purchased for using with your macramé board, although you can use your own choice of pins if you prefer.

It is possible to create elaborate pieces with a macramé board without the fuss of tangled cords, because the cords can be strategically placed in the cut-out notches, so helping you keep your work neat and tidy at all times.

You'll also find that a macramé board is large enough to accommodate several projects simultaneously. Whether you are creating one or more items, you can either attach your work with the pins provided or place the cords through the cut-out notches.

Securing cords

When it comes to creating knots on a macramé board, you may find it helpful to secure some cords at the bottom of the board as well. For example, if you secure the inner cords of a Square Knot by placing them through one of the bottom notches, you will be able to work effortlessly around them when tying your knots. Whether you need to place your outer cords over or under the inner cords, you will find that they stay securely in place if you do this, allowing you to get on with your work more efficiently.

Using the grid

Depending on what materials you are using for your project, the marked-out numerical measures can help you judge how many knots it takes to make an inch or half-inch, etc. This will give your work added precision and so help you to create a professional finish. Try making Square Knots in different thicknesses of cord and seeing how many knots are needed per inch. This will give you a good reference point for all your future projects and also help you to decide what materials to use.

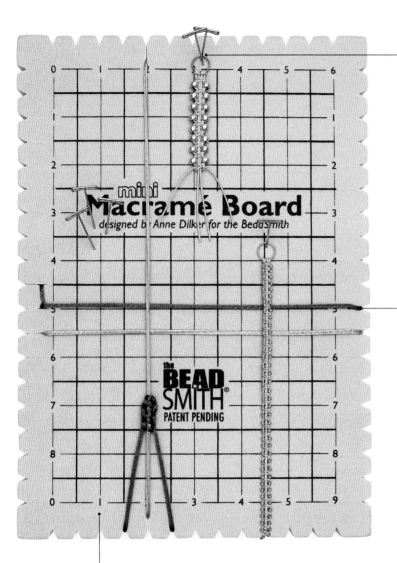

Macramé boards are made from memory foam, which is 'self-healing'. So, if you choose to use pins on your board for added security, then any holes they leave will disappear as if by magic. Specially designed, long-shanked pins can be purchased, although any pins will do.

The notches around the outside of the board make securing your cords in place a breeze. Place the cord in a notch, bring the end around to the front through the next notch, and bring the end underneath the long cord, and then back through the original notch. This cord will now be really secure. Alternatively, tie a double knot in the end of your cord and then place it in a notch. The knot will catch at the back of the board and hold the cord in place.

The grid of a macramé board is marked out in inches and half-inches, which makes it really easy to measure your jewellery piece to the correct length and ensure that the width is consistent, and the starting and ending lengths equal.

Alternatives to boards

Push pins and a corkboard can be a good alternative to a macramé board, or you can make your own board with just a few simple steps using a clipboard, a few pins and a little quilting.

Tension

Tension plays a very important role in producing perfect and professional-looking macramé. It is crucial that you try to create even and well-spaced knots throughout a piece of work. Use as many pins or tape as you wish to secure your project. A macramé board helps a lot with this, as it has cut-out notches around the edges to help keep your cords in place, but don't be afraid to use extra pins to hold your actual work in position too. Head pins and tape are useful little accessories to have to hand here.

When you are working with knots, try to pull them in a secure way, i.e. not too tight or too loose. Pulling the knots too loosely will make your work look tatty, while pulling them too tightly will not only make the piece look untidy, but you may also lose the actual design of the knot in your pattern.

You may also need to take into consideration the type of cord you are working with. For example, a silky cord may slip undone quite easily, so pulling this a little tighter may help. On the other hand, a raw cotton cord may not need as much tightening. So the advice here is to experiment with different cords and see what you prefer.

You also need to keep each knot as even as the last one and as even as the next one. Try to ensure that the knots are evenly spaced at all times. Uneven knots make macramé work look unprofessional and messy.

Practice makes perfect, but it can be much more difficult to create a perfect and even tension with some knots than others. Square Knots, for instance, are quite forgiving, but you can't get away with the same irregularities when it comes to the Diagonal Double Half Hitch Knot, as is shown in the samples below.

The basic steps for creating knots with the perfect tension are:

1 Create the desired knot by pulling the cord firmly, but not too tightly, and check that it represents a good example of the actual knot you are trying to create.

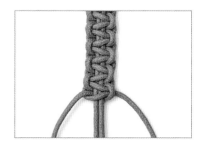

2 When performing the next knot in your sequence, check carefully that it matches the previous knot you have just created.

TOO TIGHT
Here is the alternating Diagonal Double Half Hitch Knot worked too tightly. It looks completely different from the too-loose sample and, as you can see, it has lost its pattern and looks very uneven and taut.

TOO LOOSE
Here is the alternating Diagonal Double Half Hitch Knot, worked too loosely. As you can see, the knots have not been tightened anywhere near enough and the work looks untidy.

PERFECT TENSION
Here is the alternating Diagonal Double Half Hitch Knot worked as it should be. As you can see, it creates a lovely, wavy pattern and each knot is performed in the same way. There are no tight or loose ends and, most importantly, it is even throughout.

Sealing Cords

To prevent cord ends and knots from fraying you can seal them in a number of different ways. Certain cords, such as cotton and linen, tend to fray more easily than others and that may inform your decision about which method to choose.

PVA glue or clear nail varnish

Both PVA glue and clear nail varnish can be quite helpful for sealing cords. Which you choose to use is a matter of personal choice, but both do the job in the same way. Simply dab a drop of glue or varnish onto the ends of the cords after you have finished your project.

Thread burners

Some cords call for a more secure sealing, however, and this is where a thread burner, zapper or sealer comes into play. These are great tools to have to hand when you're working with threads and cords. They can be used on synthetic cords and threads, such as nylon, and also on silk. They do not work on cotton-type threads though, so you will need to use either some glue or clear nail varnish here instead.

Thread burners have a fine, heated tip that allows for precision application with just the push of a button. They cauterize the ends of the cords and prevent them unravelling. When used to melt and fuse the ends of cords, they will stop the final knots becoming untied. Please note that it's best to let the cord melt and then push the melted end against the knot, rather than melting the knot itself. You'll find that these tools are so much more precise than using a cigarette lighter. Also, they are essential with Chinese Knotting Cord and for sliding Square Knot fastenings. As an alternative, you can use a small naked flame, but I would exercise great caution with this method.

Thread burners can be purchased from most good craft retail outlets and are usually battery operated.

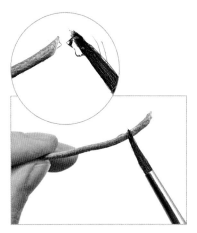

Cut your cord at a diagonal angle. Using a paintbrush, cover the final 2.5 cm (1 in) of the cord in PVA glue. Allow it to dry for at least an hour.

1 Decide where you want to seal your cord and thread it through the burner (thicker cords should be cut and sealed from the side as they would damage the zapper).

2 Hold down the activation button to heat up the wire end. Then simply pull the cord through the tip to seal the end.

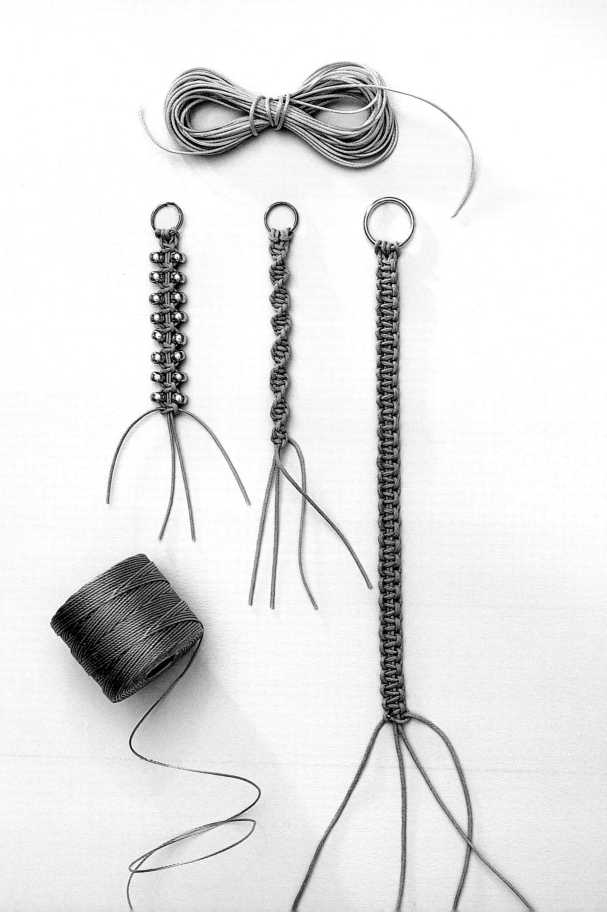

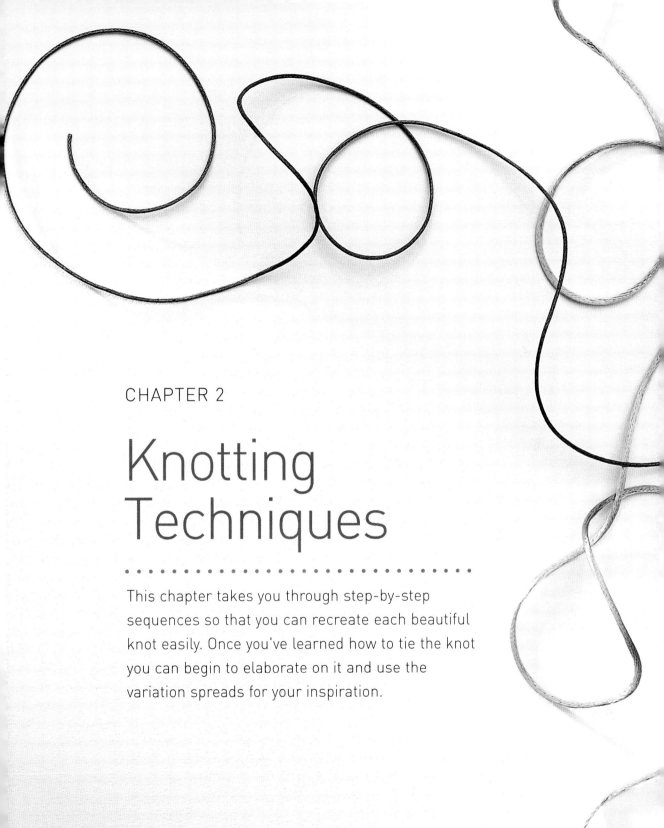

CHAPTER 2

Knotting Techniques

· ·

This chapter takes you through step-by-step sequences so that you can recreate each beautiful knot easily. Once you've learned how to tie the knot you can begin to elaborate on it and use the variation spreads for your inspiration.

Overhand and Lark's Head Knot

The Overhand Knot and Lark's Head Knot are both very simple, but versatile, knots. The Lark's Head Knot, in particular, is very useful for macramé. This knot is most often used for attaching cords to findings or other materials.

The Lark's Head Knot can be used to anchor pendants and charms, and hold them securely in place. You can also attach this knot to another cord in the same way you would to a finding (see page 69). Furthermore, it can be used to end a project, producing a nice, professional finish – although you'll need to apply some craft glue or instant glue gel to stop the knots coming apart if you use it in this way. Pulling the knots really tight is an important factor here, too.

The Overhand Knot is also very simple to create and just slips into position and ties onto itself. You can work with the Overhand Knot using several cords to create a diamond-style lace pattern, which can be used to make a gem case or to hold a small object such as a stone or cabochon (see pages 62–65).

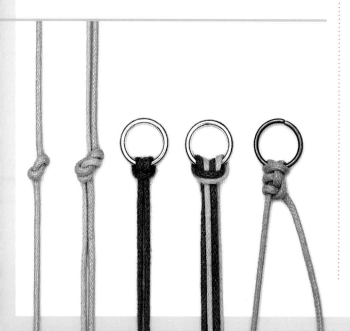

Overhand Knot

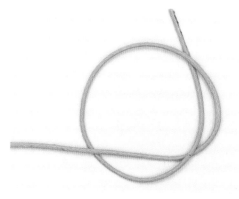

1 Make a loop with your cord by placing the left end over the right end. Pass the right-hand cord around and through the loop.

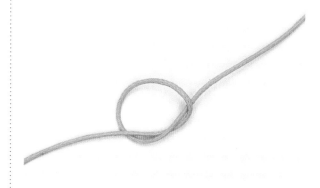

2 This knot can also be created by starting with a loop with the right cord over the left and then wrapping the left-hand cord over and through.

3 Pull the two ends to tighten the knot.

Lark's Head Knot

1 Fold the cord in half and place the folded section through the ring, as shown.

2 Pull the looped end forwards, over the ring and the cord ends. Then draw the two cord ends through the loop.

3 Pull the two ends to tighten the knot.

Vertical Lark's Head Knot

1 Fold the cord in half and attach it to your finding, or other cord, using a Lark's Head Knot. Take the right cord under and then over the left cord to create a loop. Pull the right cord through the loop.

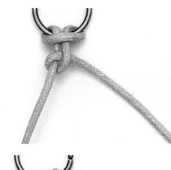

2 Pull the right cord tight to start creating the Vertical Lark's Head Knot.

3 Take the right cord over and then under the left cord, creating another loop, and pull the right cord through the loop.

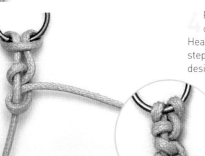

4 Pull the right cord tight to create one Vertical Lark's Head Knot. Repeat these steps until you have your desired length.

Square and Spiral Knot

The Square Knot is the basis for many different macramé patterns and so it's essential you learn how to perform this useful knot well. It is a simple, but versatile, little knot, which has many possibilities when used with different materials and beads. The Spiral Knot is simply half a Square Knot and consequently forms a wonderful spiral shape.

The Square Knot is most often used to make friendship-style bracelets, either with or without beads. Even these popular little bracelets can vary greatly, however, depending on how you use the Square Knot to attach the beads to the cords. For example, the beads can either run as a single line through the middle of the bracelet or as two lines along the outer sides.

Of course, you can also use Square Knots on their own to create bracelets with no beads at all. The Square Knot and its many variations can be used to create both multi-stranded bracelets and attractive stack bracelets. For instance, you could combine three or more strands of Square Knots to create a wonderful braided bracelet. If that wasn't enough, the simple Square Knot is often seen in many wrap bracelets and anklets.

Square Knot

1 Start with four cords. To work these onto a split ring, fold two lengths of cord in half and attach each to the split ring using a Lark's Head Knot (see page 29) to give you four working cords.

2 Place the right-hand cord over the two central 'lazy' cords and under the outer left cord. Then take the outer left cord, pass it under the two lazy cords, and pull it up through the loop on the right.

3 Pull the ends of the outer cords to tighten.

Spiral Knot

4 Place the outer left cord over the two lazy cords and under the outer right cord. Then place the right cord under the two lazy cords and pull it up through the loop on the left.

5 Pull the ends of the outer cords to tighten and complete one Square Knot.

6 Repeat Steps 2–5 until the knotting reaches the desired length.

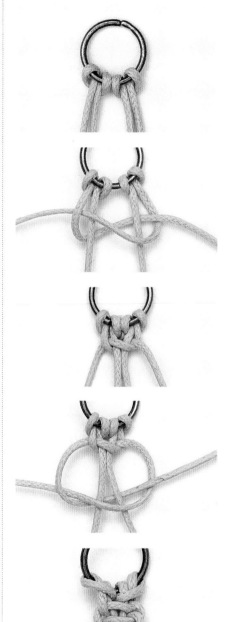

1 Start with four cords. To work these onto a split ring, fold two lengths of cord in half and attach each to the split ring using a Lark's Head Knot (see page 29) to give you four working cords.

2 A Spiral Knot is created by repeating Steps 2–3 of the Square Knot over and over again. Place the right-hand cord over the two central 'lazy' cords and under the outer left cord. Then take the outer left cord, pass it under the two lazy cords, and pull up through the loop on the right.

3 Pull the ends of the outer cords to tighten and complete one Spiral Knot.

4 Repeat Steps 2–3 until the knotting is the desired length. The tighter these knots are tied, the more attractive the finished spiral will be.

Square Knot Variations

Square Knot
using 0.6 mm
waxed cotton
cord.

Square Knot
using 0.5 mm
nylon cord.

Square Knot, with beads
threaded over the two outer
cords, using 0.6 mm
waxed cotton cord.

Square Knot, with beads
threaded over the central
cords, using 0.5 mm
nylon cord.

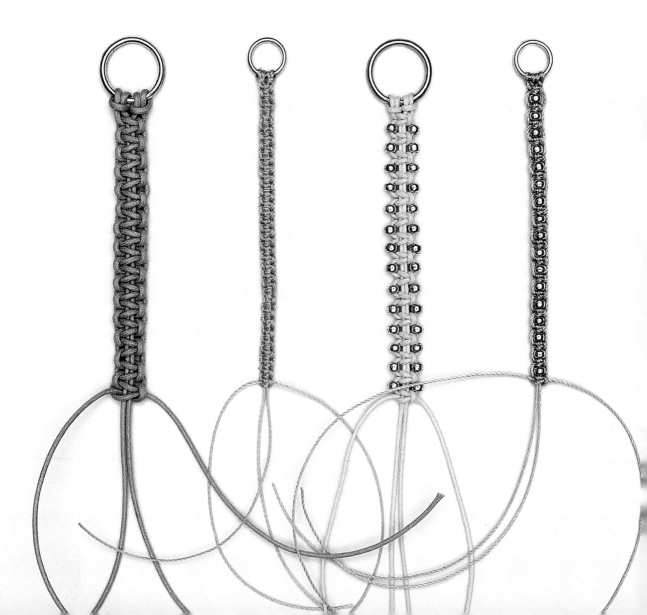

This piece of alternating Square Knot lace was created using six lengths of 0.6 mm waxed cotton cord. After attaching the cords with Lark's Head Knots, create a Square Knot using the first four cords on the left. Do the same with the next four cords and the same again with the remaining four cords. Omitting the first two cords on the left, create a Square Knot with the next four cords. Take the next four cords and create another Square Knot. Repeat this process until you have the length you desire.

Spiral Knot using 0.6 mm waxed cotton cord.

Spiral Knot using 0.5 mm nylon cord.

Spiral Knot with beads threaded over the outer cords, using 0.6 mm waxed cotton cord

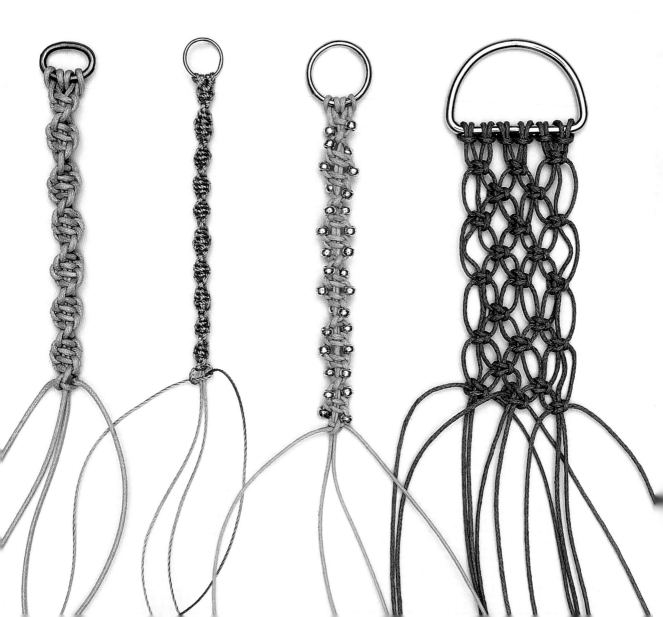

Double Half Hitch Knot

The Double Half Hitch Knot is said to be one of the most difficult macramé knots to master. It is shown here with two cords attached to a split ring, giving you four cords to work with. The Double Half Hitch Knot can be worked both diagonally and horizontally.

In very simple terms – and this is definitely something worth remembering – the Double Half Hitch Knot is created by wrapping one piece of cord around another twice. This may be either left to right or right to left.

Some very pretty, wave-style bracelets (see pages 78–80) are made by working diagonally with this knot. Tension and tidiness are both very important factors when you're working with this design and knot.

A lot of striped designs can also be created using the Double Half Hitch Knot horizontally. If you are using more than one colour in your piece, remember it is the cord that is used to 'wrap' around the 'lazy' cord that will be the colour actually on show.

To begin with, I will explain how to perform the Left Double Half Hitch Knot using the outside left cord as a lazy cord.

Left Double Half Hitch Knot

1 Start with four cords. To work these onto a split ring, fold two lengths of cord in half and attach each to the split ring using a Lark's Head Knot (see page 29) to give you four working cords.

2 Take the second cord from the left, pass it behind the left-hand 'lazy' cord, then over the lazy cord and up through the loop.

3 Now take the same cord over and then under the lazy cord, up through the second loop, as shown, and pull tight.

4 Using the third cord from the left, repeat the wrapping pattern described in Steps 2–3, still wrapping over the same lazy cord. Pull the cords tight.

5 Using the right-hand cord, repeat Steps 2–3, again wrapping over the same cord.

6 Keep knotting, repeating Steps 2–5, but now use the new left-hand cord as the lazy cord.

Right Double Half Hitch Knot

1 Start with four cords. To work these onto a split ring, fold two lengths of cord in half and attach each to the split ring using a Lark's Head Knot (see page 29) to give you four working cords

2 Take the second cord from the right, pass it behind the right-hand 'lazy' cord, then over the lazy cord and up through the loop.

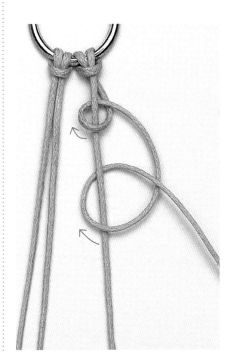

3 Now take the same cord over and then under the lazy cord, up through the second loop, as shown, and pull tight.

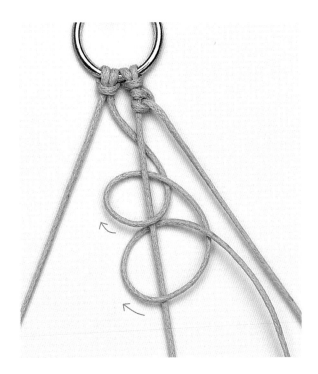

4 Using the third cord from the right, repeat the wrapping pattern described in Steps 2–3, still wrapping over the same lazy cord. Pull the cords tight.

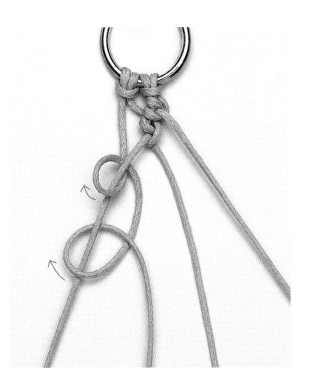

5 Using the left-hand cord, repeat Steps 2–3, again wrapping over the same cord.

6 Keep knotting, repeating Steps 2–5, but now use the new right-hand cord as the lazy cord.

Double Half Hitch Knot Variations

Left Double
Half Hitch
Knot using
0.6 mm waxed
cotton cord.

Left Double
Half Hitch
Knot using
0.5 mm nylon
cord.

Right Double
Half Hitch
Knot using
0.6 mm waxed
cotton cord.

Right Double
Half Hitch
Knot using 0.5
mm nylon
cord.

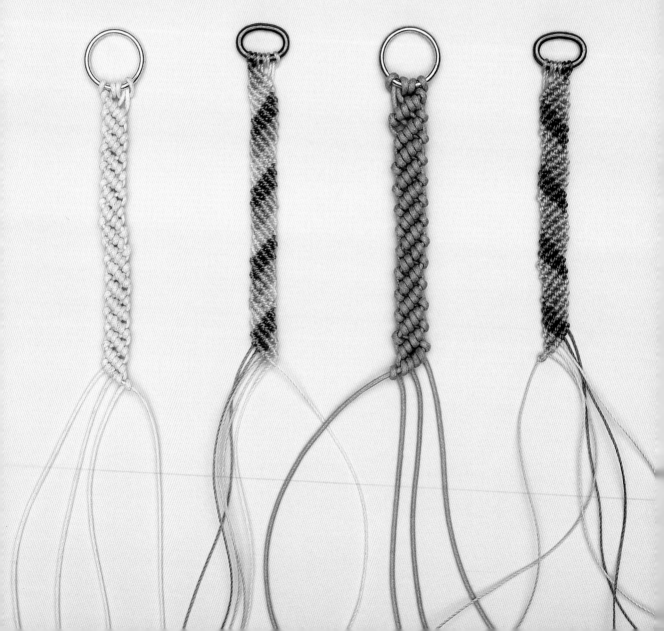

Left Double Half
Hitch Knot
threaded with
beads using
0.6 mm waxed
cotton cord.

Right Double
Half Hitch Knot
threaded with
beads using
0.6 mm waxed
cotton cord.

Alternating rows of
Right and Left Double
Half Hitch Knots
worked vertically
(simply hold the cord
you are tying onto
horizontally) using
0.6 mm waxed
cotton cord.

Alternating rows of
Right and Left Double
Half Hitch Knots worked
diagonally (simply hold
the cord you are tying
onto diagonally)
using 0.5 mm
nylon cord.

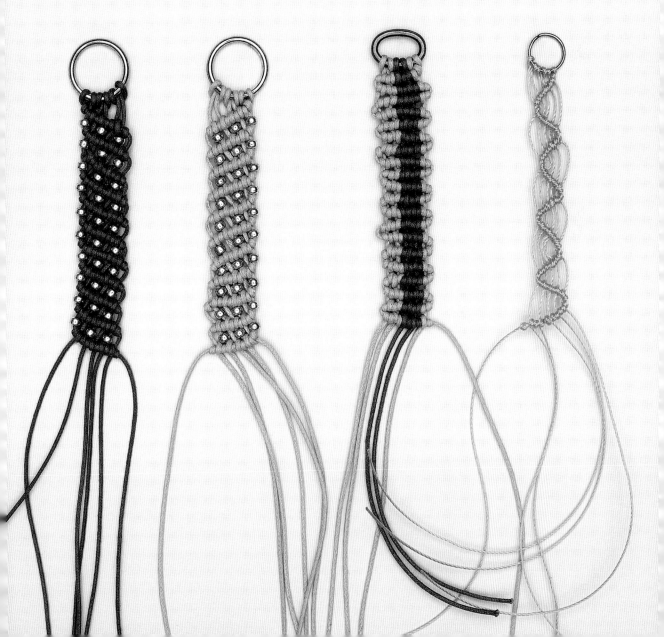

Half Hitch Knot

This macramé knot may look much more complicated than the Double Half Hitch Knot, but it is created with just a few extra steps. It can either be worked from left to right or from right to left (just like the Double Half Hitch Knot). This is another knot that is frequently used to make friendship-style bracelets.

When working a row of Half Hitch Knots you are only using one cord (the first in your row) that wraps individually across all the other cords. Wrapping the same cord over the others in this way makes that cord 'visible' in your pattern. The Double Half Hitch Knot on the other hand is used by wrapping all the cords around just one 'lazy' cord (the first in your row) making the lazy cord 'invisible' in your pattern.

Left Half Hitch Knot

1 Start with four cords. To work these onto a split ring, fold two lengths of cord in half and attach each to a split ring using a Lark's Head Knot (see page 29) to give you four working cords.

2 Place the outer left cord over and then under the next cord to its right, and pull up to make a loop. Repeat once.

3 Pull the ends of the cords to tighten the knot.

4 Repeat Steps 2–3 using the original outer left cord, but this time place it over the next free cord to the right.

Right Half Hitch Knot

This is the same as the Left Half Hitch Knot, but is worked from right to left.

2 Pull the ends of the cords to tighten the knot.

5 Keep repeating Steps 2–4 until the outer left cord becomes the new outer right cord.

1 Starting with four cords, as for Step 1 of the Left Half Hitch Knot, place the outer right cord over and then under the next cord to its left, and pull up to make a loop. Repeat once more.

3 Repeat Steps 1–2 using the original outer right cord, but this time place it over the next free cord to the left.

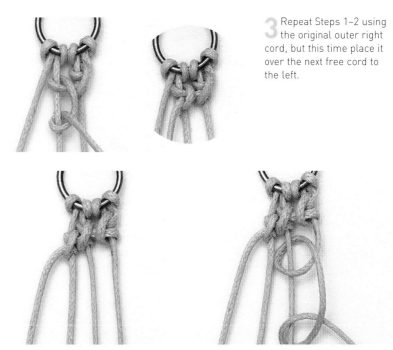

6 Then begin the pattern again using the new left-hand cord. Keep knotting in this way until you reach the required length.

4 Keep repeating Steps 1–3 until the outer right cord becomes the new outer left cord.

5 Then begin the pattern again using the new right-hand cord. Keep knotting in this way until you reach the required length.

Half Hitch Knot Variations

Left Half Hitch Knots made with four thick cords in two colours using 0.6 mm waxed cotton cord.

Left Half Hitch Knots made with six 0.6 mm cords in three.

Left Half Hitch Knots made with six thin cords in three different colours using 0.5 mm nylon cord.

Right Half Hitch Knots using two cords in 1 mm cotton cord.

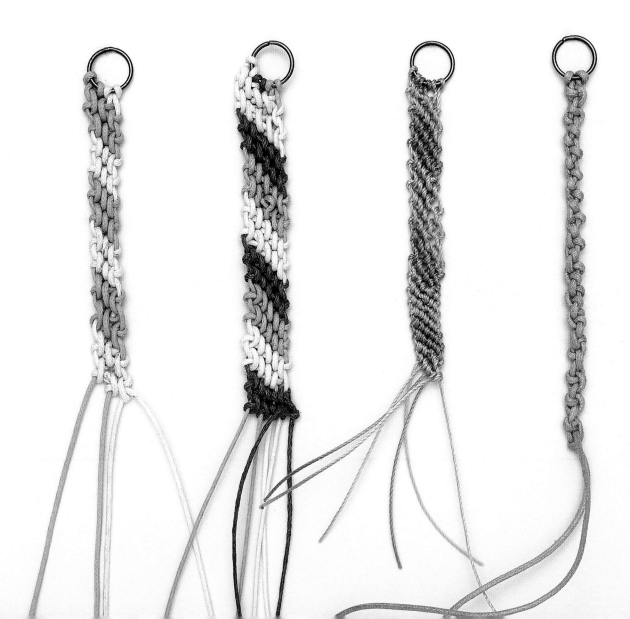

Right Half Hitch Knots using four cords in 1 mm cotton cord.

Right Half Hitch Knots made with six thin cords in three different colours using 0.5 mm nylon cord.

Right Half Hitch Knots using beads and four cords in 0.6 mm cotton cord.

Left and Right Half Hitch Knots using beads in a chevron pattern using 0.6 mm cord.

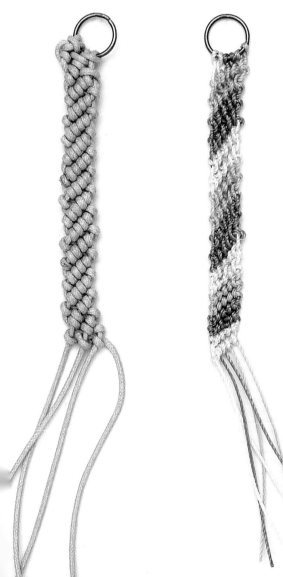
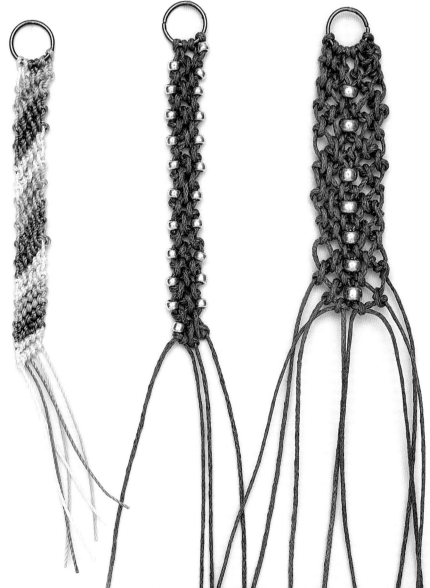

Button Knot

The Chinese have been using these perfectly round little knots as buttons for centuries; hence their name. In Chinese Buddhism, the endless pattern created by button knots represents the eternal cycle of life and it has exactly the same symbolic meaning in Celtic mythology.

Button knots are very useful for making knotted jewellery. They look especially good when used with lampwork beads, which have large holes that are perfect for the 2 mm satin cords usually used for the knotting. It is not advisable to make Button Knots using thin cords because they would be too small to be noticeable.

It is a good idea to complete this knot on a macramé board, with the help of a few pins.

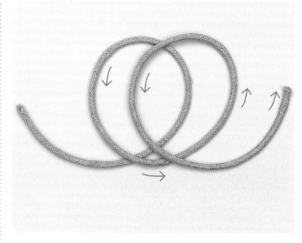

1 Place a length of cord, measuring 60 cm (24 in), on the macramé board. Keeping the left-hand side of the cord very short and the right-hand side longer, make one loop with the right cord on top of the left cord. Make an identical loop, again using the right cord on top of the left cord, ensuring that it overlaps the first loop to create three spaces (as shown). You may find it helpful to pin the length of cord to the board where necessary to keep it even (not many pins will be needed for this).

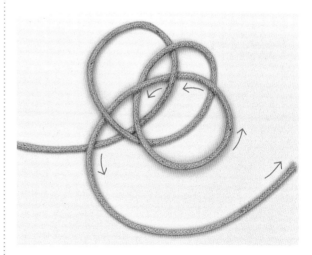

2 Take the long right cord down through the right-hand space, up through the middle space, and then down through the left-hand space. Pull the cord through to the left, just enough to make a new loop on the right-hand side (the knot should resemble a pretzel).

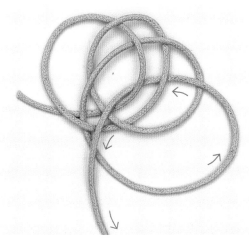

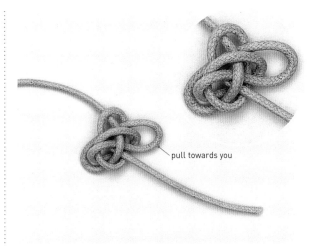

pull towards you

3 Take the long cord around to the right again, thread it down through the new loop, then up again through the central loop and towards you. Try to keep the loops fairly small and more or less equal in size, because this will help the tightening of the knot in the next step.

5 You'll see that the loops are uneven, with some of them being longer than others, so these must be pulled through to tighten the knot. To do this, hold the knot in your left hand and pull one loop (it does not matter which one) towards you until it is tight. The next loop will now be too large, so pull it through as you did for the first loop. Make sure you always follow in the same direction. Continue pulling the excess loops through the knot (there are eight loops in total) until you reach the end and the knot looks almost round.

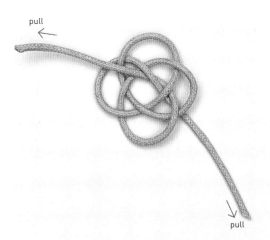

pull

pull

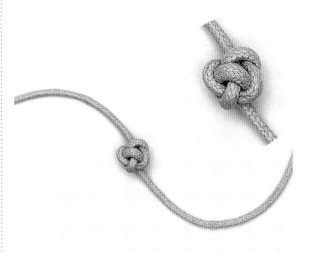

4 Now carefully remove the knot from the board. Pull the cord you have been working with towards you and hold the short cord you started with in Step 1 behind the knot and pull this away from you. The knot should resemble the photograph in Step 5.

6 You may find that the knot still needs some 'tweaking' to make it nice and round and even. When you are finished, it should look like the photograph above.

Button Knot Variations

Button Knots using three 2 mm nylon satin cords in different colours, with each of the colours tied in succession around the other two.

Button Knots using two 2 mm nylon satin cords in different colours tied together. Includes a bead after every second knot.

Button Knots tied using 2 mm nylon satin cords in sequence, with a square bead added between each group of three knots.

Button Knots using two 2 mm nylon satin cords in different colours, with each cord tied around the other, then divided and knotted singly (so the Button Knots in each colour sit side by side). These groups of Button Knots alternate in sets of three, with beads added in between.

A series of Button Knots using two 2 mm nylon satin cords in different colours, with knots and beads on each side, gathered together with two Dew Knots (see pages 48–49).

Two dyed 1.5 mm braided nylon cords in the same colour, positioned side by side, with groups of three beads on each, and gathered together with a Button Knot (one cord is tied around the other).

Two 1.5 mm braided nylon cords in the same colour, positioned side by side. The cords are threaded horizontally in opposite directions through the beads and then gathered together with a Button Knot (made with one cord tied around the other).

Series of Square Knots (see pages 30–31) using two 2.5 mm rayon satin cords in different colours. Then Button Knots using two cords in the same colour tied together, with beads on the cords beside the knots, at intervals of three Square Knots.

Snake Knot

The snake is one of the twelve animals in the Chinese Horoscope. It is considered to be a bringer of good fortune.

The Snake Knot is sometimes called a Dew Knot, because a series of Dew Knots makes a Snake Knot. The Dew Knot has a very simple interlocking design that uses two cords – and is very versatile.

The series of Dew Knots that makes up a Snake Knot is shown here using satin cords. These are softer than waxed cotton cord and show the knot sequence very clearly.

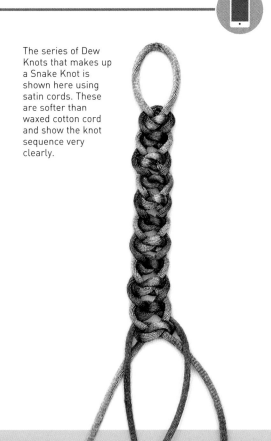

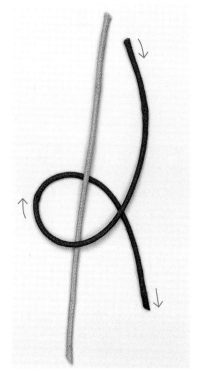

Dew Knot

1 Start with two cords (or one cord folded in half). Take the right-hand cord (shown here in dark blue), pass it over the left-hand cord, up and to the right, and under the left-hand cord to make a loop. Then pass the right-hand cord under itself and down.

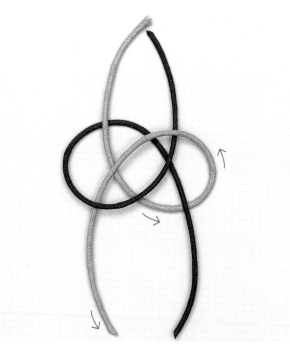

2 Take the left-hand cord (shown here in light blue) and make another loop by passing it under the right-hand cord, up and over the right-hand cord, and then down over itself and under the dark blue left loop.

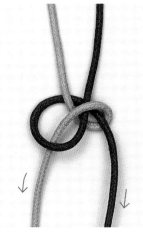  

3 Holding the cords at the top with one hand, pull the light blue cord down first and then the dark blue cord to make a knot.

4 The tightened knot should like the photograph above and is called a Dew Knot. If you are using this knot to attach two cords, tie two Dew Knots, one closely behind the other, because this will be more attractive and stable.

5 A series of Dew Knots tied closely together is called a Snake Knot.

Snake Knot using Alternating Colours

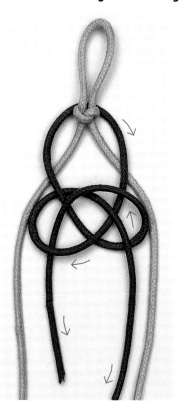

6 A second cord in another colour can be added to the Snake Knot at the beginning. Fold the cord in two and make a Dew Knot in one colour (shown here in light blue) and tighten it. Then add a second cord in another colour (shown here in dark blue), starting above and behind the first knot with a folded length of cord. Bring the new cords down and over the first cords, as shown. Make another Dew Knot, but do not tighten it too much, otherwise you will lose the shape of the sequence of knots.

7 Continue in this way, making Dew Knots in the alternating colours, until you reach the required length for the piece.

Snake Knot Variations

A continuous series of Dew Knots made with 1 mm Korean knotting cord to create a Snake Knot.

A Snake Knot made from a series of Dew Knots in 1 mm Korean knotting cord, with seed beads added after every four Dew Knots.

A Snake Knot sinnet made from continuous Dew Knots using 2 mm nylon satin cords in two colours, with intermittent beads.

Four 2 mm nylon satin cords in two colours. Two consecutive Dew Knots are tied on the right and left sides, then the two central cords are tied into Dew Knots, thus creating a net-like pattern which is known as alternating Dew Knots.

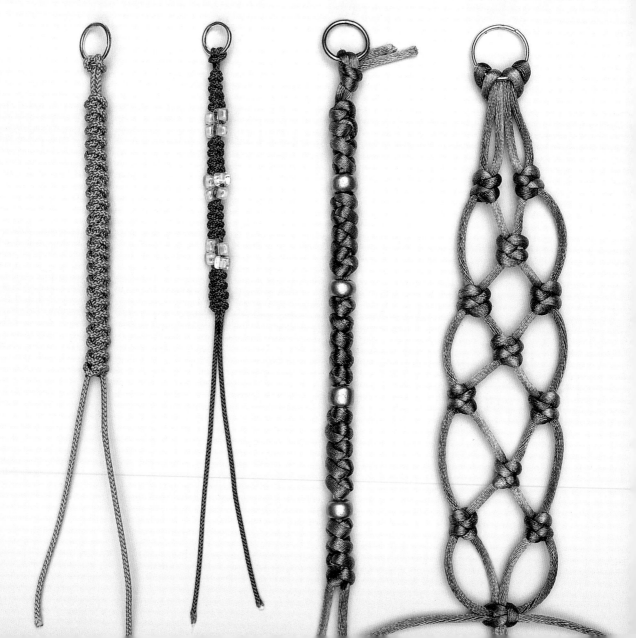

Dew Knots made with doubled 2 mm nylon satin cords. Bead added, then the two cords on each side have been knotted with alternating Double Half Hitch Knots (see page 34–37), followed by another bead. This sequence is repeated once.

Snake Knot made with a series of Dew Knots using doubled 2 mm nylon satin cords. Seed beads are added after every three knots.

2 mm nylon satin cords in two colours are used to make alternating Dew Knots. The knots are tied fairly loosely to create an intertwined braid. Beads have been added to the sides in the central section.

Sets of two Dew Knots, separated by two 2 mm nylon satin cords in different colours, with three seed beads threaded onto each cord. This sequence is repeated several times.

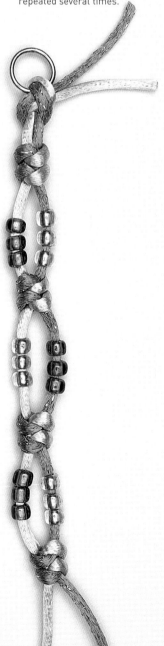

Double Coin Knot

The shape of the Double Coin Knot resembles two overlapping coins and denotes prosperity. In the West it is known as a Josephine Knot, and it's symmetrical, interlocking design is similar to that of a traditional Celtic knot.

The Double Coin Knot is very versatile, and can be tied both horizontally (using one cord end) and vertically (using two cord ends). The instructions given here show how to create both a Right- and Left-hand Double Coin Knot. You'll need to alternate these knots if you decide to create a vertical length. If you only made a series of right-hand knots, the whole piece would twist and not lay flat at all.

Right-hand Double Coin Knot: side-by-side knots

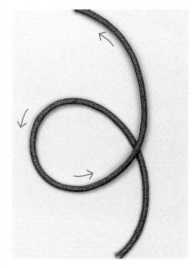

1 Pin the non-working end of the cord to the board. Make a left-facing loop by looping the 'working' end of the cord up, around and over itself, and around to the left.

2 Bring the working end of the cord further around to the left and down.

Left-hand Double Coin Knot: side-by-side knots

1 Pin the non-working end of the cord to the board. Make a right-facing loop by looping the 'working' end of the cord up, around and over itself, and around to the right.

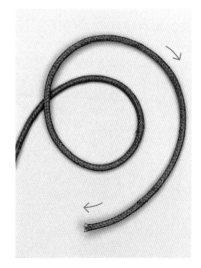

2 Bring the working end of the cord further around to the right and then down.

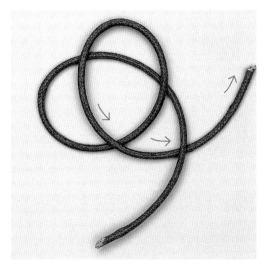

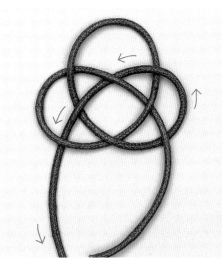

3 Now lay the cord over the top of the loop and pass it under the beginning cord, as shown. Bring the cord end upwards.

4 Bring the working end of the cord up, towards the left, then down, weaving it over, under, over, and then under the cords it crosses. The knot is now finished and will stay in place due to the alternate weaving over and under at the intersections.

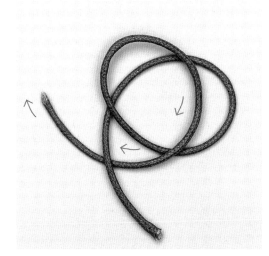

3 Now lay the cord over the top of the loop and pass it under the beginning cord, as shown. Bring the cord end upwards.

4 Bring the working end of the cord up, towards the right, then down, weaving it over, under, over, and then under the cords it crosses. The knot is now complete and will stay in place due to the alternate weaving over and under at the intersections.

Double Coin Knot Tied with Two Cords: vertical series of knots

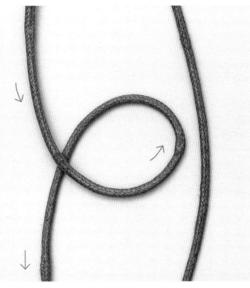

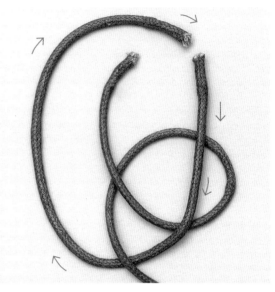

1 Place two cords side by side. Make a loop with the left-hand cord, with the end of the working cord passing underneath itself, as shown. Pin into position.

2 Bring the right-hand cord down so that it crosses over the top of the loop, then pass it underneath the left-hand cord, as shown above, and bring it upwards. Use more pins to keep the cords in place.

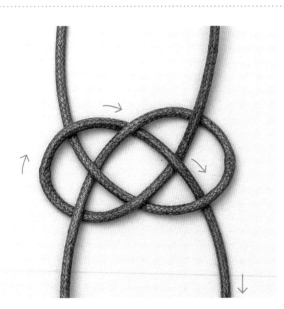

3 Bring the working cord around and down over the top of the left-hand cord. Now weave it downwards under, over, and then under the looped cords it crosses. The knot is now completed.

4 Tighten the knot and leave the cord ends to point downwards ready to make another knot underneath, but this time with the 'unders and overs' reversed.

5 Here is an example of the same knot tied with two cords, except the 'unders and overs' are the opposite of the previous knot (in Step 4). This is important to remember because in a vertical sequence of Double Coin Knots every knot should be the reverse of the one above. If all the knots were exactly the same, then the sequence of knots would twist and not lie flat.

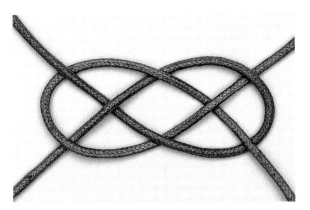

6 This photograph shows how the knot looks when it is tied with the two cords coming from the sides, making an attractive centrepiece for a braid. Two separate cords can be interlinked permanently when the knot is tied like this – some people call this a True Lovers Knot.

Double Coin Knot Variations

A series of Double Coin Knots made with two 2 mm nylon satin cords in different colours. The knots are made vertically, with one sitting beneath the other.

Doubled 1 mm Korean knotting cord started in the middle with a sideways intertwined Double Coin Knot. There are two more Double Coin Knots tied one above the other on each side of this central knot. The piece is finished with a bead, some Square Knots (see pages 30–31) and a ring at the top and with another bead at the bottom.

Square Knots (see pages 30–31) are tied using 1 mm nylon satin cords around two 25-cm (10-in) pieces of 1 mm Korean knotting cords using two different coloured cords. The resulting braids are used to make three vertically tied Double Coin Knots that are attached to a closed jump ring with more Square Knots.

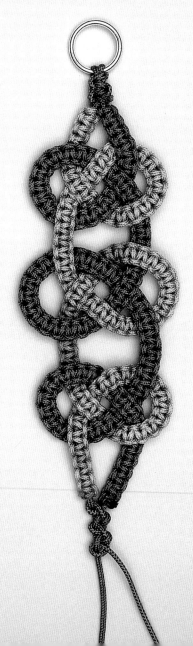

A series of Double Coin Knots made with two pieces of 1.5 mm leather cord in different colours, with one knot sitting below the other.

Lark's Head Knots (see page 29) are tied vertically, using 1 mm nylon satin cord, around a 20-cm (8-in) length of 1 mm Korean knotting cord and then the new braid is tied into a Double Coin Knot. The 'tail' is made of Square Knots (see pages 30–31), with a single bead in between.

A series of sideways Double Coin Knots, tied with two 2 mm nylon satin cords at once, using just one end of the cords and following the pattern.

Celtic Square Knot

Celtic knots are distinctive due to their flowing curves and repetitive patterns. The loops are interlaced and the crossings alternate between going over the top and underneath each other. This simple knot is a perfect example of the graceful curves of a Celtic knot: the cords flow under and over each other to make a stable and perfectly symmetrical knot.

The monks of early Christianity used knot patterns when decorating manuscripts, to fill squares in their designs. This knot fills a square beautifully and looks lovely made in cord. In order to help your knot retain its shape, coat one side of it in diluted PVA glue.

1 Use a piece of cord measuring approximately 50 cm (20 in) in length. Fold the cord in half and pin it to the macramé board.

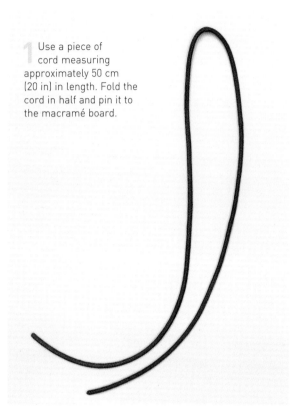

2 Make a loop using the left-hand cord, with the end passing underneath the main cord. Leave the end pointing downwards, diagonally and towards the right.

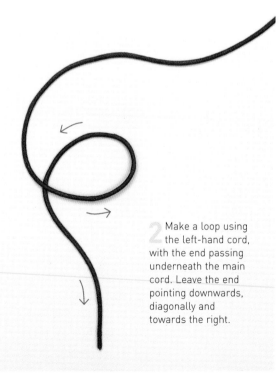

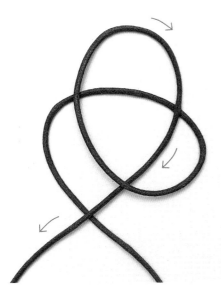

3 Take the right-hand cord and – now on the left of the loop – thread it downwards over, under and over the left-hand cord loops, as shown above.

5 Now take the cord down, through the lower right-hand loop, passing it under and then over the cord. Tidy up the knot and make sure it is symmetrical. At this stage you can adjust the size of the knot, or add a second or third cord if you wish.

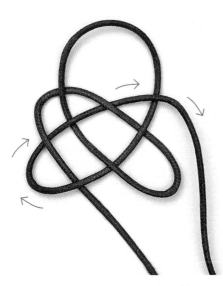

4 Loop the same cord to the left and thread it upwards, taking it under, over, under and over the existing loops.

6 Tighten the knot if needed by gently pulling the loops through, starting at the lower end of the knot and working on each side separately.

Celtic Square Knot Variations

A series of Celtic Square Knots made with three 1 mm Chinese knotting cords in two different colours and finished with Square Knots (see pages 30–31). Beads are used between each Celtic Square Knot.

Celtic Square Knot made with two 2 mm satin cords in different colours. Finished at the top and bottom with Square Knots (see pages 30–31) and seed beads.

Two Celtic Square Knots made with two 2 mm satin cords in different colours and separated by Chinese Dew Knots (see pages 48–49).

Single Celtic Square Knot made with 1 mm Chinese knotting cord. The cord used to make the knot was first tied with vertical Lark's Head Knots (see page 29). The piece is finished with a sequence of Square Knots (see pages 30–31) and eight seed beads around a central bead.

Single Celtic Square Knot made with 1 mm satin cord. The cords were first tied with Alternating Half Hitch Knots (see pages 40–41). The four cords at the top were then tied into Square Knots (see pages 30–31) above the Celtic Square Knot (with a single bead in between), with the same pattern worked on the other side of the Celtic Square Knot.

Single Celtic Square Knot made with Lark's Head Knots knotted sinnet (see page 29), with Square Knots (flanked by two beads) and finished with Alternating Half Hitch Knots (see pages 34–37).

Wrapping a Stone

Wrapping a stone using only Overhand Knots is a simple procedure. In this example, I have chosen macramé cord in an orchid colour to complement the grey stone. In general, you can choose any cord from the many different types available, because most cords are suitable for this purpose. However, it is advisable not to use a very thick cord with a very small stone.

The first loop at the top allows you to attach the netted stone to a necklace or other item of jewellery. The tassels at the bottom can be trimmed to any length.

When you are working with this pattern – and pairing up the cords – you need to remember to pair up the cords to create a diamond shape. For this reason, it's a good idea to splay out the cords when you're working so that you can see clearly which cords you are pairing up.

1 Take four cords, fold them in half and make one Overhand Knot (see page 28). This will give you eight working cords.

2 Spread out the cords, and begin to knot pairs together using an Overhand Knot.

3 Pair up the rest of the cords and tie each one together with an Overhand Knot.

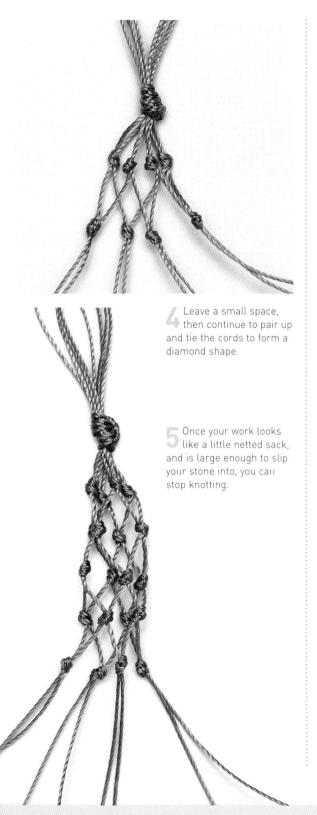

4 Leave a small space, then continue to pair up and tie the cords to form a diamond shape.

5 Once your work looks like a little netted sack, and is large enough to slip your stone into, you can stop knotting.

6 Slip the stone into the case and then tie together tightly with a final Overhand Knot bringing all the cords together.

Wrapping a Cabochon

There are many different methods for wrapping a cabochon, such as using glue to fix the cabochon to some felt then attaching a piece of macramé work to it. However, I would like to demonstrate a completely micro-macramé way of doing this. I have also chosen to use beads because I personally think this results in a tidier and more professional look. It also spaces out the knots nicely and highlights the cabochon as well. It can, of course, be done without the beads if you prefer.

I have chosen Alternating Lark's Head knots made with thin 0.6mm cotton cord because of the ability of this knotting to stretch. This is a useful quality when it comes to wrapping it around the cabochon in the final step. Size 8 seed beads have also been selected, as the size 11 ones are too small to thread onto this cord. You will need to be familiar with working a Lark's Head Knot vertically to be able to create this knot.

1 Using three cords in different colours, take the first cord and make a Lark's Head Knot (see page 29) over the third cord.

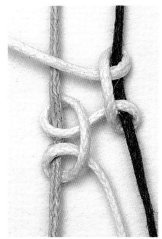

2 Take the first cord again and make another Lark's Head Knot, but this time over the second cord.

3 Thread a size 8 seed bead onto the third cord.

4 Use the first cord again to make another Lark's Head Knot over the third cord. Then thread another seed bead onto the second cord.

5 Repeat Steps 2–4 until your work is just a fraction shorter than the perimeter of your cabochon.

6 Wrap your work around the cabochon, pulling it very tight, and finish by tying all the ends together with an Overhand Knot (see page 28). Pull tightly once more.

Wrapped Stone and Cabochon Variations

Netted stone using 0.5 mm
nylon cord and beads.

Netted stone using 0.6 mm
waxed cotton cord.

Netted stone using
0.6 mm waxed cotton cord
in two different colours.

Large wrapped cabochon using 0.6 mm waxed cotton cords in two different colours, without beads.

Large wrapped cabochon using 0.6 mm waxed cotton cord in a single colour with beads.

Small wrapped cabochon using 0.6 mm waxed cotton cord in a single colour, without beads.

Finishing a Project

There are a multitude of ways in which you can finish a macramé project. Deciding which method to use largely comes down to personal preference, but you'll also need to take into account the style of the piece you're making. You can attach lots of different findings to your work, or you could opt for a method that does not involve using findings at all.

Attaching jump rings

In many cases, you will need to add a jump ring (see pages 14–15) before adding a clasp to finish your work. Here's the most effective way to do this.

1 Hold the jump ring on either side of the opening using two pairs of pliers.

2 Do not pull the ring apart, as this will distort the shape and the ring will not close properly again. Use one pair of pliers to hold the jump ring and the other to push the other half of the ring backwards.

3 Thread the terminator finding and, if applicable, the fastening – for example, a lobster clasp – onto the open jump ring, then move the pliers in opposite directions to close the ring.

Attaching terminators and clasps

Crimps, cord ends and ribbon ends come in many shapes and sizes (see pages 14–15) but are all fixed in place by applying pressure with pliers. This fold-over cord end has a central section with a tab on each side. The cord is inserted into the central part of the clamp and the tabs are then folded over the top.

1 Snip off the excess cord once you have finished your piece of macramé work, then place the end of the cord in the central part of the cord end finding.

2 Use a pair of flat-nose pliers to fold in one side of the finding and hold the cord in place. Fold in the other side of the finding so that it overlaps the first slightly.

3 Attach a jump ring and your chosen clasp (see above) to complete the finish.

Finishing with Lark's Head Knots

This is a very tidy way to finish your macramé projects and can often look very professional. This finishing option may prove a little more tricky than other methods, but you should find that it becomes much easier once you have practised the technique a few times.

1 Attach your cords to a split ring, as shown, using Vertical Lark's Head Knots (see page 29).

2 Pull the cords very tight and dab clear PVA glue or instant glue gel on the knots to keep them secure.

3 Once the glue is dry, snip off the excess cords.

Using a bead and loop

For this finishing method you will have to create a length of macramé that's long enough for you to make a loop at the start of your work which can accommodate a bead.

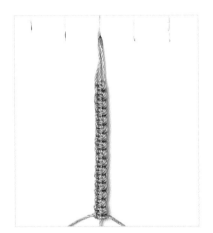

1 Measure out your cords and place half of them through a notch on the macramé board. Create a length of Square Knots (see pages 30–31) that is twice the length of your bead.

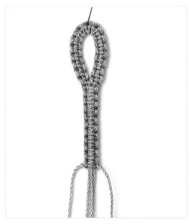

2 Remove the cords from the notch. Fold the knotted length in half and pin it to the board. Now work all of the cords together in a series of Square Knots until you reach the desired length.

3 Thread on the bead, tie off the piece with an Overhand Knot (see page 28), and snip off the excess cords.

Simple Sliding Knot

This simple and very effective Sliding Knot makes your bracelet or necklace length adjustable and also free from metal closures, which is ideal for those who are allergic to metal. It is basically an Overhand Knot (see page 28), made with two loops instead of one, which is tied around the opposing cord so that it slides along the cord. The opposite free end is then tied around the opposite cord in the same way, so that it also slides.

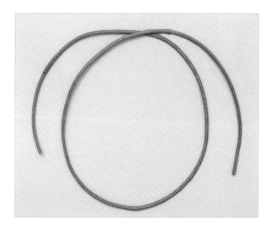

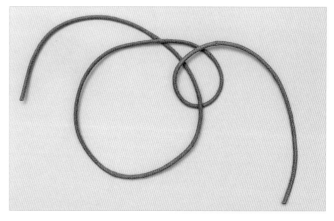

1 Leave at least 16 cm (6 in) of extra cord on each side of the point at which you want the necklace or bracelet to be the longest. That is, the necklace should go over your head easily and the bracelet should fit over your hand and wrist when you put it on. Place the cord on the macramé board so the ends are pointing in opposite directions, with the cord on the right-hand side looping over the cord on the left-hand side, as shown.

2 Use the right-hand cord to make another smaller loop, passing it first under and then over the opposite cord, as shown.

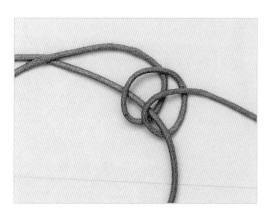

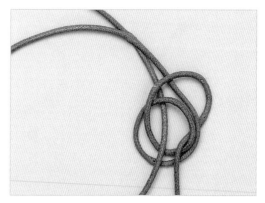

3 Repeat Step 2 to make another identical loop below and beside the first loop.

4 Push the two loops together and then bring the end of the right-hand cord through both of the loops, threading from the back to the front.

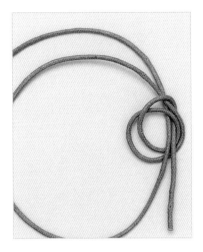

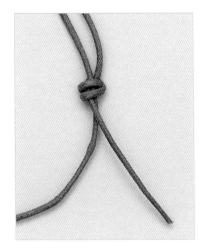

5 To tighten the knot, pull the end of the cord while you are holding the other side of the knot. (Take care not to hold the cord around which your knot is being tied.)

6 Your Sliding Knot is now tightened and will slide along the opposite cord. Trim the extra cord end. If you wish to glue the knot, make sure you glue the end to the knot and avoid getting any glue on the cord that needs to slide!

7 Turn the necklace or bracelet around and then repeat the pattern exactly to create another Sliding Knot on the other side. Trim the extra cord and glue carefully, if necessary. The two knots will slide easily and the necklace or braclet can be made to the length you need.

Using tassels

A trendy way of finishing a macramé bracelet is to use tassels.

Simply tie an Overhand Knot (see page 28) at the end of your work, leaving enough cord for you to tie the bracelet at the back of the wrist.

Using braids

This finishing method means that you can dispense with attaching findings. It's also a lovely way to complete delicate, friendship-style bracelets.

Braid a length of the leftover cords so that it is long enough to reach around your wrist. Finish with an Overhand Knot (see page 28) and snip off the excess cords.

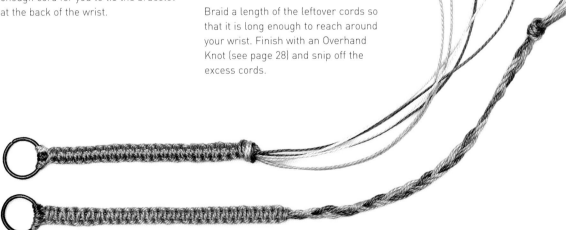

CHAPTER 3

Projects

· ·

The following projects introduce some great ideas
for turning your new macramé craft skills into
wonderful jewellery. With this selection of different
jewellery projects you'll be amazed at how cords
can be transformed into beautiful gifts.

Lacy Watch Strap

This pretty watch strap is created with alternating Square Knots (see pages 30–31). It is a lot easier to make than you might think, so have a go and you'll be pleased that you did.

Materials Needed

* 8 lengths of 0.7 mm waxed cotton cord, measuring approx. 61 cm (24 in)
* 1 x watch face
* PVA glue or instant glue gel
* 2 x 16 mm ribbon ends
* 2 x 6 mm jump rings
* 1 x lobster clasp

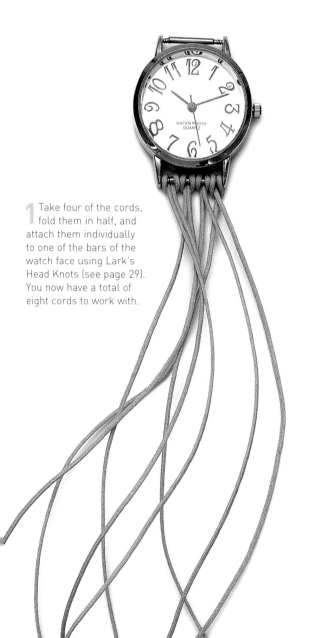

1 Take four of the cords, fold them in half, and attach them individually to one of the bars of the watch face using Lark's Head Knots (see page 29). You now have a total of eight cords to work with.

2 Using the first four cords on the left, perform one Square Knot (see pages 30–31).

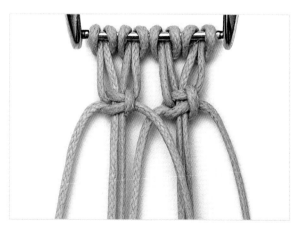

3 This time using the next four cords on the bar, perform another Square Knot.

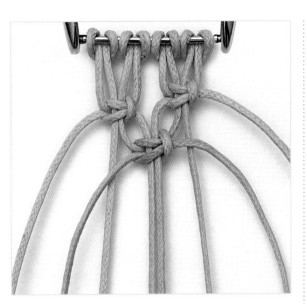

4 Now take the four central cords and perform another
Square Knot.

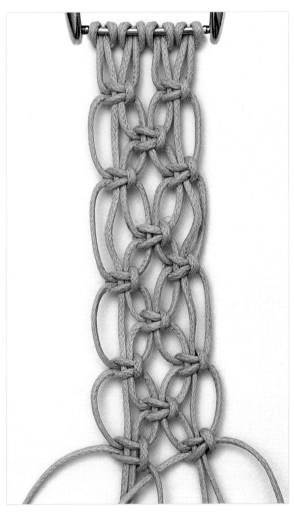

5 Repeat Steps 2–4 until your work measures
approximately 8 cm (3 in) in length.

7 Snip off the excess cords then finish off one end of the watch strap by dabbing some glue onto the cord ends before attaching a ribbon end, jump ring and lobster clasp (see page 68).

6 Attach the remaining four cords to the bar on the other side of the watch face (as in Step 1) and repeat Steps 2–5 to create the rest of the watch strap.

8 Repeat Step 7 at the other end of the watch strap, but omit the lobster clasp.

Wave Bracelet

An eye-catching and beautiful little bracelet that is made using diagonal Double Half Hitch Knots and a few pretty beads.

Materials Needed
* 5 lengths of 0.5 mm nylon cord, measuring approx. 152 cm (60 in)
* 1 x 10 mm split ring or closed jump ring
* PVA glue or instant glue gel
* 1 x 16 mm ribbon end
* 1 x 6 mm jump ring
* 1 x lobster clasp

* Depending on your wrist size and the tension of the bracelet, you will also need:
  Approx. 126 size 8 seed beads in Colour A
  Approx. 133 size 8 seed beads in Colour B
  Approx. 56 size 6 seed beads

1 Fold each cord in half and attach them individually to the split or closed jump ring using Lark's Head Knots (see page 29).

2 Starting on the right, and working from right to left, work two rows of diagonal Right Double Half Hitch Knots (see pages 36–37).

3 Working from left to right, thread the following beads onto the following cords:

Cord 1: One size 6 seed bead
Cord 2: Three size 8 seed beads in Colour A
Cord 4: Six size 8 seed beads in Colour B
Cord 6: Nine size 8 seed beads in Colour A
Cord 8: Thirteen size 8 seed beads in Colour B
Cord 10: Seven size 6 seed beads and six size 8 seed beads in Colour A in an alternating fashion.

4 Starting on the left, and working from left to right, work two rows of diagonal Left Double Half Hitch Knots (see pages 34–35).

5 Working from right to left this time, thread the following beads onto the following cords:

Cord 1: One size 6 seed bead
Cord 2: Three size 8 seed beads in Colour A
Cord 4: Six size 8 seed beads in Colour B
Cord 6: Nine size 8 seed beads in Colour A
Cord 8: Thirteen size 8 seed beads in Colour B
Cord 10: Seven size 6 seed beads and six size 8 seed beads in Colour A in an alternating fashion.

6 Repeat Steps 2–5 until your work measures around 15 cm (6 in) in length.

7 Snip off the excess cords and finish the bracelet by applying a few dabs of glue to the cord ends before attaching a ribbon end, jump ring and lobster clasp (see page 68).

Chevron Cuff

This trendy cuff with its attractive chevron pattern is quite quick and simple to make. If you wish, you can add more cords to make a wider cuff or fewer cords to make a slimmer one. The choice is yours.

Materials Needed
* 2 lengths of 0.6 mm waxed cotton cord, measuring 229 cm (90 in), in Colour A
* 2 lengths of cord, measuring 229 cm (90 in), in Colour B
* 1 length of cord, measuring 229 cm (90 in), in Colour C
* 1 x 15 mm split ring or closed jump ring
* PVA glue or instant glue gel
* 1 x 16 mm ribbon end
* 1 x 6 mm jump ring
* 1 x lobster clasp

1 Fold all the cords in half and attach them individually to the split or closed jump ring using Lark's Head Knots (see page 29) in the following order:

First: Colour A
Second: Colour B
Third: Colour C
Fourth: Colour B
Fifth: Colour A

2 Using the first five cords on the right, and working from right to left, perform a row of diagonal Right Double Half Hitch Knots (see pages 36–37).

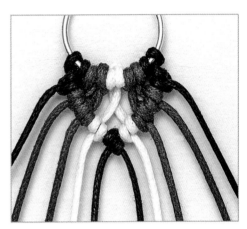

3 Using the first five cords on the left, and working from left to right, perform a row of diagonal Left Double Half Hitch Knots (see pages 34–35).

4 Tie the two inner cords together with another Left Double Half Hitch Knot.

5 Repeat Steps 2–4 until your work measures approximately 18 cm (7 in), or is the desired length for your macramé piece.

6 Snip off the excess cords and finish the bracelet by applying a few dabs of glue to the cord ends before attaching a ribbon end, jump ring and lobster clasp (see page 68).

Celtic Square Knot Earrings

These Celtic Square Knot earrings are formed using Lark's Head Knots tied in a series around a vertical cord to make a lovely flat braid. The resulting knotted length lends itself beautifully to being shaped into curves and loops.

Materials Needed
* 50 cm (20 in) of 0.9 mm C-Lon Tex 400 cord
* 225 cm (89 in) of 0.5 mm C-Lon cord (i.e. regular thickness) in the same colour
* Macramé board (or cork mat) and pins
* Yarn bobbin
* Adhesive tape
* 2 size 6 cube-shaped TOHO seed beads (TOHO seed beads have larger holes)
* Ear wires
* Instant glue gel

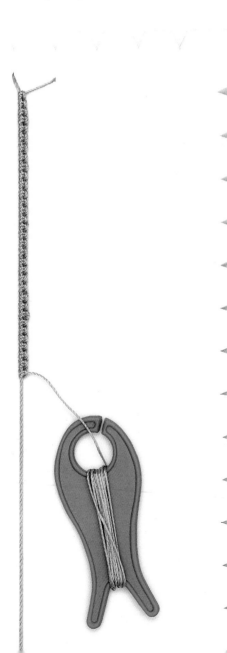

22 cm (8¹⁄₂ in).

1 Attach the length of C-Lon Tex 400 cord to the centre of the macramé board, securing it in the slots at the top and bottom of the board (see page 23).

2 Attach one end of the length of C-Lon cord to the yarn bobbin with a small piece of adhesive tape, then wind the cord around the bobbin until you have only 25 cm (10 in) of the cord remaining. The bobbin makes it much quicker and easier to create the series of Lark's Head Knots.

3 Attach the free end of this 25-cm (10-in) length of cord to the top of the board, winding it around a couple of notches to keep it securely in place.

4 Use the longer cord to tie a series of Vertical Lark's Head Knots around the cord on the board (see page 29), until your knotting measures 22 cm (8¹⁄₂ in).

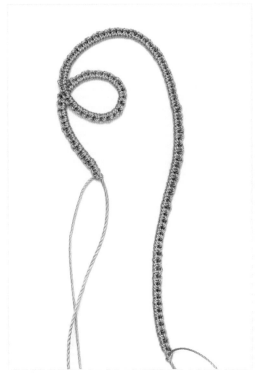

5 Remove the knotted length from the board then pin it back onto the board at the halfway point and on the right-hand side, as shown. The knotted side should be facing outwards. Do not cut or trim any cords at this stage.

6 Make a loop with the knotted cord on the left-hand side by passing the end under the main cord, to begin the Celtic Square Knot (see pages 58–59). Add more pins, as necessary, to keep the knotted length of cord in place.

7 Take the right-hand end of the knotted cord and weave it downwards through the loop, passing it over, under, and over the cords it crosses, as shown.

8 Bring the same knotted cord towards the left and back up again, then weave it under, over, under, and over the cords that it crosses.

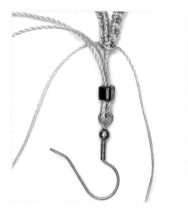

9 Then bring the same cord to the right and downwards before threading it through the lower right loop, first under and then over. This is the time to remove some of the pins, apart from the central one at the top (i.e. the halfway point) because this will help keep the knot even on both sides.

10 Bring the two knotted sides together and make one Square Knot (see pages 30–31) with the outside knotting cords around the two thicker central cords, to hold them together. Thread the two thicker central cords through a size 6 seed bead. Then thread an ear wire onto the two central cords.

11 Fold the two central cords upwards and thread them back through the seed bead as shown.

12 Pull up and tighten the central cords until the ear wire is sitting next to the seed bead, leaving 4 mm between the bead and the end of the knotting. Put a spot of instant glue gel between the top and bottom central cords above the bead and glue them together.

13 Trim off the extra lengths of cord, then make more Square Knots around the glued-down central cords. This will secure and hide the cord ends. You will probably only need one or two Square Knots to reach the bead.

14 Put another spot of instant glue gel on the cords on each side, close to the knotting. When the glue has dried thoroughly, trim the excess cords as close to the knotting as possible. Repeat for the second earring.

Double Coin Knot Bracelet

The Double Coin Knot is named because of its likeness to two overlapping coins. Double Coin Knots look lovely when tied one after the other to make a bracelet. In Chinese culture, multiple Double Coin Knots are associated with prosperity!

Materials Needed
* 5 m (197 in) of 1.5 mm waxed cotton cord, cut into 4 pieces measuring 1.25 m (49 in) each
* Macramé board (or cork mat) and pins
* Toggle clasp (with a loop large enough for two cords to go through)
* Instant glue gel
* Diluted PVA glue (1 part glue to 6 parts water)
* Small paintbrush

1 Slide two pieces of cord into one slot of the macramé board (see page 23, leaving approximately 12.5 cm (5 in) of cord behind the board. (This is for attaching the toggle later on.) Slide the other two cords into a slot two slots away from the first set of cords, again leaving 12.5 cm (5 in) behind the board.

2 Holding the right-hand cords together, make a loop following the instructions for tying a Right-hand Double Coin Knot (see pages 52–53). Make sure that the downward left-hand cords are sitting on top of the loop, as shown, then bring them under the right-hand cords, up and around.

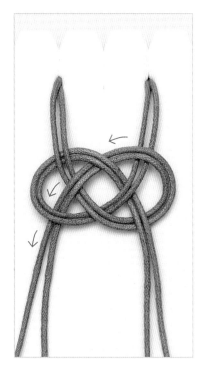

3 Bring the left-hand cords up and over the right-hand cords and then down to the left again, weaving the cords under, over, and then under the left side of the knot, as shown above.

4 Tighten the knot slowly, working from the top down, until it reaches the size you want for the bracelet.

5 Make a Left-hand Double Coin Knot (see pages 52–53) below the first knot. Alternating the knots in this way keeps the bracelet flat; if the knots were all made in the same direction, the bracelet would twist.

6 Continue making alternate Right- and Left-hand Double Coin Knots until the bracelet is long enough to fit around your wrist (you'll need about nine or ten knots for the average wrist). Don't forget to allow some space for the toggle closure as well – approximately 5 cm (2 in) should be sufficient. Bring all four cords together and make a very loose Square Knot (see pages 30–31) with the two outside cords around the two central cords. Thread the two central cords through one half of the toggle clasp.

7 Bring the two threaded central cords up and then thread them through the centre of the Square Knot, as shown.

8 Dab a couple of spots of instant glue gel in the space between the folded central cords. Quickly tighten the Square Knot and make another Square Knot below it – as you tighten the Square Knots, you help keep the glued cords well bonded. Put a spot of instant glue gel on all four of the long cord ends that need trimming, just next to where they exit the knots. When the glue is thoroughly dry, trim off the extra cords close to the knots (it will be almost invisible).

9 Turn the bracelet around, so that the unfinished end is at the bottom of the board. Attach the other half of the toggle clasp to the unfinished end exactly as you did for the first half of the toggle in Steps 6–8. Apply some diluted PVA glue with a brush to one side of the bracelet to keep the knots in place. The glue might make the cords look a shade darker, but this won't matter because it is on the back of the bracelet.

Macramé Ring

This cute and fun little macramé ring is easy to create and can be made to look very different if you use a range of colours and stripe widths.

Materials Needed
* 4 lengths of 0.5 mm nylon cord, measuring approx. 102 cm (40 in), in Colour A
* 3 lengths of 0.5 mm nylon cord, measuring approx. 102 cm (40 in), in Colour B
* Adhesive tape
* Bulldog clip (optional)
* Thread burner

1 Lay out all the cords in Colour A and all the cords in Colour B, then secure them with some adhesive tape, leaving about 8 cm (3 in) of cord above the tape. You might also find it helpful to secure your work with a bulldog clip for the first couple of stages.

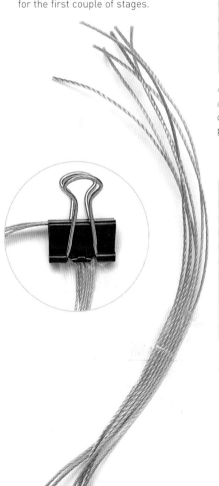

2 Starting from the left, and working from left to right, perform a row of Left Double Half Hitch Knots (see pages 34–35).

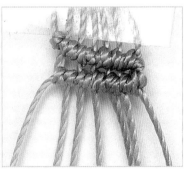

3 Starting from the right this time, and working from right to left, perform a row of Right Double Half Hitch Knots (see pages 36–37).

4 Repeat Steps 2–3 until your work measures around 5½ cm (2¼ in), or is slightly larger than the diameter of your finger.

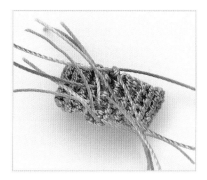

5 Fold your work in half, remove the tape, then tie each of the opposite cords together individually with two Overhand Knots (see page 28).

6 Snip off the excess cords and use the thread burner to carefully cut the knots and seal the cord ends. Turn the ring inside out (which means it will now be the right way round) to complete one macramé ring.

Index

Credits

All step-by-step and other images are the copyright of Quarto Publishing plc. While every effort has been made to credit contrbutors, Quarto would like to apologise should there have been any omissions or errors –and would be pleased to make the appropriate correction for future editions of the book.

Author acknowledgments

I would like to thank my editor Chelsea Edwards for her support and guidance in the creation of this book, it has been a great pleasure to work with her and the staff at Quarto.

Suzen Millodot

Video links

Each QR code, once scanned with your smartphone, will link to the tutorial for the knot listed beside it. Simply download a free app to scan, if needed, and check out the short videos to help you perfect the knot.

Square Knot

Double Half Hitch Knot

Half Hitch Knot

Snake Knot

Double Coin Knot

If you would prefer to view the videos on your computer you can type the folliwing URL addresses into your internet browser and access the content that way.

Square Knot: http://qr.quartobooks.com/macj/clip1.html
Double Half Hitch Knot: http://qr.quartobooks.com/macj/clip2.html
Half Hitch Knot: http://qr.quartobooks.com/macj/clip3.html
Snake Knot: http://qr.quartobooks.com/macj/clip4.html
Double Coin Knot: http://qr.quartobooks.com/macj/clip5.html

101st AIRBORNE
MARKET GARDEN 1944

Steven Smith and Simon Forty

Casemate
PHILADELPHIA & OXFORD

Published in the United States of America and Great Britain in 2016
by CASEMATE PUBLISHERS
1950 Lawrence Road, Havertown, PA 19083
and 10 Hythe Bridge Street, Oxford, OX1 2EW

ISBN-13: 978-1-61200-423-5

Produced by Greene Media Ltd.

Cataloging-in-publication data is available from the Library of Congress
and the British Library.

10 9 8 7 6 5 4 3 2 1

Printed and bound in China
For a complete list of Casemate titles please contact:
CASEMATE PUBLISHERS (US)
Telephone (610) 853-9131, Fax (610) 853-9146
E-mail: casemate@casematepublishers.com

CASEMATE PUBLISHERS (UK)
Telephone (01865) 241249, Fax (01865) 794449
E-mail: casemate-uk@casematepublishers.co.uk

Acknowledgments
Most of the photos are US Signal Corps images that have come from a
number of sources. Grateful thanks go to BattlefieldHistorian.com, NARA
College Park, MD, and the George Forty Library for historic photos; other
credits are noted on the photographs—WikiCommons has proved
extremely useful. If anyone is missing or incorrectly credited, apologies:
please notify the authors through the publishers.

I'd like to thank in particular Tom Timmermans and Battledetective.com for
the Then and Nows. Other thanks are due to Leo Marriott, Peter Hendrikx,
Mark Franklin (maps), Ian Hughes (design) Richard Wood and the military
cyclists (particularly Peter Anderson) for photos and enthusiasm.

Previous page:
The 101st Airborne monument, Eindhoven. Alex P. Kok/WikiCommons
(CC BY-SA 3.0 NL)

Right:
Men of the 506th PIR at the edge of Son woods (Zonsche Forest).
Note the second man's SCR-300 radio.

Contents

Introduction

OPERATION MARKET GARDEN, which involved the largest airborne operation of all time, was a daring attempt by the Western Allies to throw a sudden left hook across the Rhine, outflank the Germans from the north, and perhaps end World War II by Christmas 1944.

After the German front in Normandy finally collapsed that August, after ten weeks of ferocious battle, the Allies enjoyed a heyday such as they had not yet seen in the war. The once-fearsome enemy was in full retreat, scrambling pell-mell across northern France and Belgium to escape to the relative safety of their Westwall along the German border. Anglo-American motorized columns pursued them just as rapidly, liberating city after city en route, including Paris, Brussels and Antwerp.

But as the Germans fell back closer to their sources of reinforcement and supply, the Allies began to outdistance their own, thanks to the continued grip Hitler held on the Channel ports. Allied armored formations began literally running out of gas, even as the prospect of another dismal European winter neared.

Into this dilemma stepped the usually cautious British Field Marshal Bernard Montgomery with a daring plan. He would launch the newly formed First Allied Airborne Army to lay a carpet of nearly 40,000 paratroopers and glidermen across Holland, to seize consecutive highway bridges and hold open a highway corridor for the British Second Army to vault across the Lower Rhine, outflanking the Westwall from the north. While Supreme Allied Commander Eisenhower favored a "broad front" strategy, and Monty's rival, George Patton, clamored for resources of his own, it was agreed to try the bold single thrust that might end the war quickly. The fact that on September 8 Germany's first V-2 rockets began firing on London, from Dutch soil, may have influenced approval for Monty's plan.

Two US airborne divisions were employed, the 101st and 82nd, along with the British 1st Airborne and the 1st Polish Independent Parachute Brigade. The simultaneous land thrust would be made primarily by British XXX Corps across the airborne carpet, flanked by the XII Corps on the left and the VIII Corps on the right. There were five major bridges to be seized by the advance paratroopers as well as a number of smaller ones, with the crucial— and farthest—crossing to be seized by the British paras over the Rhine itself, at Arnhem. Upon viewing the plan, 1st Airborne's commander, Roy Urquhart, did wonder if they might be going "a bridge too far."

Montgomery's HQ was optimistic, however, expecting that if the 101st Airborne executed its tasks along the corridor from Eindhoven to Veghel, and the 82nd could seize its bridges farther north, from Grave to Nijmegen, the armored columns would reach Arnhem in two days. The enemy appeared to be already on the ropes, hardly able to hold a front, and elite divisions of paratroopers landing in their rear areas would sow chaos, allowing for the full-blooded thrust of armor to quickly cut through.

Operation Market Garden ("market" for the airborne assault, "garden" for the land attack) would commence on September 17, 1944. It has since been called "a magnificent disaster," as the armor would never reach Arnhem, and the British 1st Airborne would be practically wiped out. As for the corridor that was to be secured in advance, the Screaming Eagles of the 101st Airborne Division coined their own term for it: "Hell's Highway."

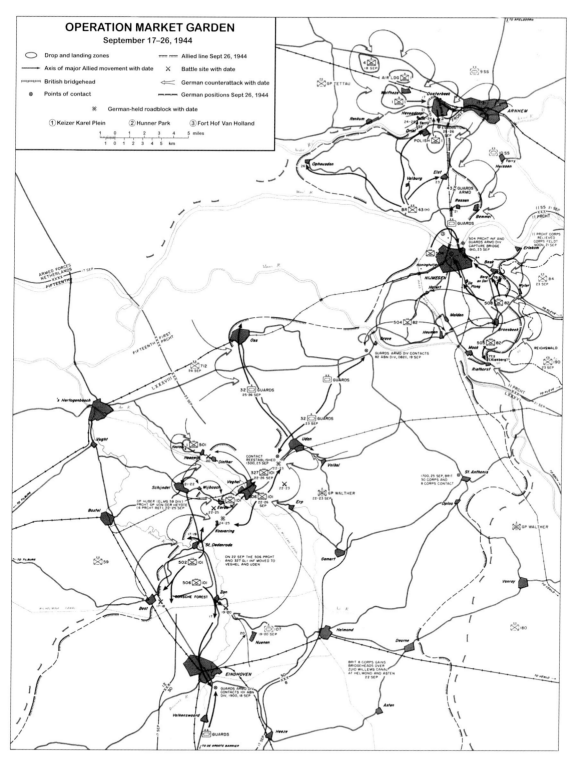

The plan looked good in September 1944. As Charles B. MacDonald put it, "The principal objective of the operation was to get Allied troops across the Rhine. Three main advantages were expected to accrue: cutting the land exit of those Germans remaining in western Holland; outflanking the enemy's frontier defenses, the West Wall or Siegfried Line; and positioning British ground forces for a subsequent drive into Germany along the North German plain."

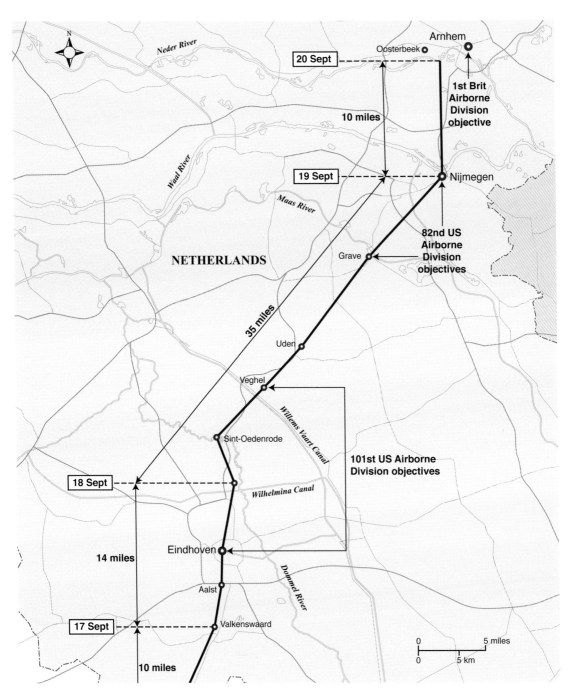

The German response to Market Garden was effective. As Robert Kershaw's excellent *It Never Snows in September* identifies, Allied historians are quick to identify mistakes rather than examine the remarkable German achievement. The real reason the operation failed was that the Germans were able to flood reinforcements into the area faster than the Allies. Some of this was fortuitous: 107th Pz Bde formed in Poland and spent six weeks training. Between August 14 and September 1 it received 154 SdKfz 251s, 36 Panther Gs, and 11 Jagdpanzer IV L/70s. Commanded by Lt-Col. Berndt-Joachim Freiherr von Maltzahn, it traveled west to Venlo between September 16–18, ordered to help defend the Westwall near Aachen. Maltzahn arrived on the evening of the 17th and was immediately instructed to use what forces he had at his disposal to attack the 101st Airborne at Son.

101st AIRBORNE ORDER OF BATTLE

CG: Maj-Gen. Maxwell D. Taylor   Asst CO: Brig. Gen. Gerald J. Higgins

Div Troops
HQ and HQ Company
801st Ordnance Company
426th Quartermaster Company
101st Signal Company
Military Police Platoon
Reconnaissance Platoon

101st Airborne Division Infantry
501st PIR (attached from Jan. 44)
502nd PIR
506th PIR
327th GIR
401st GIR

101st Airborne Division Artillery
HHB Div Arty
321st Glider Field Artillery Battalion
377th Parachute Field Artillery Battalion
463rd Parachute Field Artillery Battalion
907th Glider Field Artillery Battalion

101st Parachute Maintenance Battalion
326th Airborne Engineer Battalion
326th Airborne Medical Company
81st Airborne Antiaircraft Artillery Battalion
101st Counter Intelligence Corps Detachment

Attached troops
BR 44th Armd Regt (BR 4th Armd Bde)
    19 Sept–25
Sept 44
BR 13/18 Hussars (BR 79th Armd Div)
    18 Oct–22 Oct 44
BR 53rd Rcn Regt (BR 53rd Div) 5 Oct–6 Oct 44
BR A&B Sqns Royal Scots Greys 6 Oct–7 Oct 44
BR 61st Rcn Regt 6 Oct–12 Oct 44
BR C Sqn Royal Scots Greys 6 Oct–17 Oct 44
BR 4th RHA Field Arty Regt (RA) (Mecz)
    12 Oct –18 Oct 44
BR 147th Field Arty Regt from 18 Oct
BR C Sqn 61st Rcn Regt 10 Oct–12 Oct 44
BR 53d Rcn Regt (BR 53d Div) 13 Oct–19 Oct 44

Battle Casualties, June 6–August 17, 1944

During Operation Market Garden the 101st Airborne Division suffered 2,110 casualties (315 killed, 1,248 wounded, and 547 missing). During the nearly two months it remained in Holland defending the Island it sustained nearly 1,200 more, in addition to increasing non-battle losses as the weather got wetter and colder and the men had to live in self-dug, frontline foxholes for much of that time.

During the war, and particularly right after it, the American Graves Registration Command was the most active and best-funded organization of its kind in history. The US was determined to find, identify, and honor all its fallen on foreign soil, and AGRC teams did repeated sweeps of northern Europe for years after the war.

Families were given the option to request the return of their soldiers' remains back to the States, which over half of them did. It was also a conviction among the Americans never to bury their dead on a former enemy's ground, and as opposed to the British practice, for example, of burying their dead near the many battlefields where they fell, the Americans set up central cemeteries.

In Holland this is the Netherlands American Cemetery at Margraten, a 75-acre plot marked by a soaring monument in the far south of the country just east of Maastricht near an ancient Roman road. There lie 8,302 U.S. soldiers, not only from Market Garden but from battles in northern Germany. There are also walls marked with the names of the 1,722 U.S. servicemen who remain listed—despite the best efforts of the AGRC—as still "missing."

Lt-Col Robert G. Cole died on September18 just before his award of the CMH for action in Normandy. He is buried at Margraten (see also p.62). *NL Wammes Waggel/ WikiCommons (CC BY-SA 3.0)*

Above:
The stage. The Dutch countryside between Eindhoven and Nijmegen is flat and crossed by many waterways.

Left:
The weather. The timetable of the airborne drop and its resupply was at the mercy of the elements. In practical terms what it meant to 101st Airborne was no artillery for two days—and a delivery time of seven days for the whole division. The longer it took to complete the air drops, the longer the 101st had to weaken its offensive capabilities by defending the DZ/ LZs.

Below left:
The locals. *Dolle Dinsdag* (Mad Tuesday)—is what the Dutch call September 5, 1944—the day that expectation outran reality. After a broadcast by the Prime Minister-in-exile, many thought that liberation was at hand, and this was even before Operation "Market Garden" started. It wasn't, of course, and many parts of the Netherlands had to wait for the end of the war in May 1945, but the overwhelming delight expressed by the Dutch as the Allies arrived caused some problems—mainly crowded streets impeding vehicle movements.

Above:

There's a lot of baloney talked about the involvement of the Dutch resistance in the operation and how far it was trusted—mainly down to the usual Montgomery bashers. There was an active, well-organized Resistance in the Netherlands, although the military didn't always trust these uncoordinated groups who often seemed at odds with each other. To help cooperation, the various divisions in the operations were assigned Jedburgh teams—that of the 101st being codenamed "Daniel II." Additionally, five Royal Dutch commandos were attached for linguist support. Daniel II comprised: British Maj. Wilson, the commander, and Sgt. Mason, the radio operator; and Dutch-speaking Lt. Dubois, and Sgt. Fokker. In practice, some Dutch citizens, including members of the Eindhoven Resistance, attached themselves to the 101st and were used as interpreters,

guides and in a counter-intelligence role to identify collaborators. The photo shows Partisan Action Nederlands member helping identify map locations.

Below:

The opposition. The excellent *www.go2war2. nl/* website discusses why the Germans fought with such tenacity across the Netherlands. Three main points are identified: first, propaganda and education—many German soldiers still believed in ultimate victory, with the V weapons helping foster this belief. Second, honor and duty—even against the sternest odds, officers and men felt (as did their opponents) that they couldn't let their mates down. Third, and some would say the biggest difference between the two sides, the summary justice meted out to those who would not fight.

1. SOETERBEEK BRIDGE, EINDHOVEN
2. EINDHOVEN LIBERATION MEMORIAL
3. 101st MEMORIAL SEAT, NEUNEN
4. SON BRIDGEHEAD MEMORIAL
5. FOUNTAIN, RADHUISPLEIN, SON
6. MONUMENT, ZONHOVE, SON
7. MEMORIAL SEAT, SON
8. AIRBORNE SOLDIER, SON
9. JOE MANN MEMORIAL, BEST
10. JOE MANN PELICAN MEMORIAL, BEST
11. COL ROBERT COLE MEMORIAL, BEST
12. WINGS OF LIBERATION MUSEUM, BEST
13. SCREAMING EAGLE PARACHUTE, PAULUSHOEVE

14. WOLFSWINKEL (COL TAYLOR'S HQ)
15. WATERHOEF FARM TEMPORARY CEMETERY MONUMENT
16. MEMORIAL TO DUTCH DEAD FROM 101st VETERANS, ST. OEDENRODE
17. CASTLE HENKENSHAGE (COL TAYLOR'S HQ)
18. OLD MILL, DE KOEVERING
19. 501st PIR PLAQUES, OLD MILL, EERDE
20. 501st GERONIMO MEMORIAL, EERDE
21. KANGAROO MEMORIAL, VEGHEL
22. KLONDIKE, COL JOHNSON (501st PIR), VEGHEL
23. KASTEEL HEESWIJK: LT-COL SAMPSON 101st CHAPLAIN, MEMORIAL; 501st PIR MEMORIALS
24. HEESWIJK MEMORIAL STATUE
25. SCREAMING EAGLE, DORPHUIS, SLIJK-EWIJK
26. 501st PIR, THE INCREDIBLE PATROL MEMORIAL, ELST
27. MAJ OLIVER HORTON PLAQUE, OPHEUSDEN
28. FIRST AID POST, OPHEUSDEN
29. TOWN HALL SCREAMING EAGLE AND PLAQUE, OPHEUSDEN
30. SCREAMING EAGLES MEMORIAL, HETEREN

Left:

The battlefield today showing the main memorials, museums, and locations of interest. Holland is very aware of the events of September 1944. Indeed, the Orange Lanyard (*Oranje Erekoord*) was awarded to the Divisional Colors of the 101st Airborne Division and all individual members who served in the Arnhem operations in the period from September 17 to November 28, 1944.

Right:

Once on the ground, the paras used whatever they could lay their hands on. Here, Dutch farmers Driek Eykemans and Toon Wervoort give the glider men a lift. The pipe smoker is Japp Bothe, one of the five Dutch Commandos of No. 2 (Dutch) Troop of No. 10 (Inter Allied) Cdo attached to the 101st. (See also caption p.9.) Veghel, September 18.

Below:

A follow-on photo to that on pp.2–3. Men of 506th PIR gather at Merks Farm before heading off towards Son Bridge, all the while watched by civilians.

From Carentan to Eindhoven

I**N ITS FIRST BATTLE**, beginning in the early morning hours of D-Day, June 6, 1944, the 101st Airborne Division covered itself in glory. Due to darkness and enemy anti-aircraft fire, the paratroopers were dropped across 20 miles of Normandy countryside, sometimes on top of enemy units or in flooded areas, but usually in small, isolated units. The result was a kaleidoscope of combat on all sides as the Germans reacted in turn to the assault.

That morning the seaborne invasion of Hitler's Fortress Europe commenced, and with daylight the 101st troopers began to coalesce and seek out their objectives: the bridges and crossroads across which German reinforcements must flow if the invasion were to be defeated on the beaches.

After two days of combat the 101st was still the only advanced infantry in its sector so was ordered to seize the key city of Carentan, which sat as a hinge threatening to divide the US front. The Germans also realized the importance of the town and held it with their own elite paratroopers, Fallschirmjäger Regiment 6,

reinforced by SS troops and armor. Outnumbered and outgunned, the 101st nevertheless outfought the enemy, until when it was just on the point of breaking in the face of massive counterattacks, the US 2nd Armored Division arrived as reinforcement.

For the rest of the month the Screaming Eagles manned defenses in the Cotentin Peninsula until being pulled into reserve, and in mid-July were withdrawn to England, less nearly 4,000 casualties (868 dead, 2,303 wounded, and 663 missing). Arriving back at their bases in southern England, the men were issued seven-day passes, while their officers sought to hastily train thousands of new recruits to re-fill the ranks.

From August to early September, after the German front in Normandy had broken, the 101st was repeatedly put on alert for another mission, but each time the Allied ground forces advanced so fast that an airborne drop proved unnecessary. Operation Market Garden, however, would prove to be no false alarm.

Right:
101st *en route* to their June 6 drop. The bazooka man is Bob Noody of the 506th PIR.

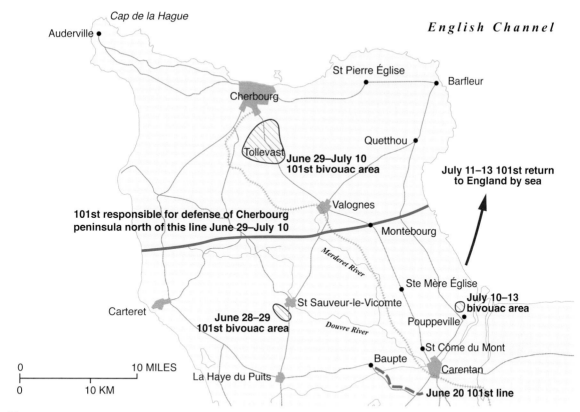

English Channel

Cap de la Hague

Auderville •

St Pierre Église

Barfleur

Cherbourg

Quetthou

Tollevast **June 29–July 10
101st bivouac area**

**July 11–13 101st return
to England by sea**

Valognes

**101st responsible for defense of Cherbourg
peninsula north of this line June 29–July 10**

Montebourg

Merderet River

Ste Mère Église

Carteret

St Sauveur-le-Vicomte

**July 10–13
bivouac area**

**June 28–29
101st bivouac area**

Douvre River

Pouppeville

St Côme du Mont

Baupte

Carentan

0 _____ 10 MILES

0 _____ 10 KM

La Haye du Puits

June 20 101st line

Above:

Clearing the Cotentin. After holding the German counterattack at Carentan, the 101st was involved in less onerous duties, moved first to St. Sauveur and then Tollevast, after the fall of Cherbourg.

Right:

After securing the beachhead, the 101st pushed FJR6 out of Carentan. The counterattack by battlehardened Fallschirmjäger and Panzers of the 17th SS pressed hard until the timely arrival of 2nd Armored. Here an M7 Priest of the 14th FA Battalion, 2nd Armored Division in Carentan.

13

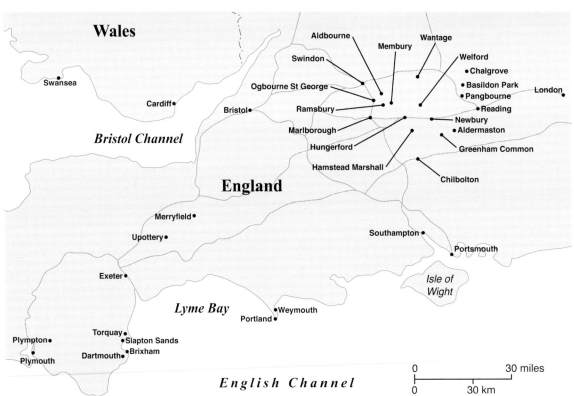

Opposite, above:
It was at Tollevast that Gen. Bernard Montgomery presented Gen. Maxwell Taylor with the British Distinguished Service Order for his bravery.

Opposite, below:
The key locations in southern England associated with 101st Division's time there.

Right:
Training with paradropped artillery.

Below:
Practice drop on Newbury.

This spread:

Practice makes perfect. Before operations in Normandy and Holland, the 101st Airborne trained and practiced. Here, men of the 377th Parachute Field Artillery Bn are put through their paces. Scheduled to be dropped on D+2, September 19, the 377th set up their firing positions at the LZ and provided much-needed support to the infantry as they faced counterattacks by strong German forces: for example, against an attack on D+3 against 1st Bn 506th PIR near the Son bridge. By D+5 they were at St. Oedenrode supporting the 501st, and on D+10, still at St. Oedenrode, they were supporting the 502nd.

Getting There

Oᴺ ᴛʜᴇ ᴍᴏʀɴɪɴɢ of September 17, 1944, the skies over England were smothered by the most immense armada of airplanes ever seen—wave after wave of bombers, transports, gliders, and fighters, as history's greatest airborne operation commenced.

The 101st's bases were centered around historic Newbury, 60 miles west of London. Just outside the town was the airfield at Greenham Common (where Eisenhower made his famous visit to 101st troopers on the eve of D-Day) with other airfields of IX Troop Carrier Command scattered among the villages of West Berkshire and Wiltshire counties. While 101st officers favored setting up their headquarters in local manor houses, the troopers themselves were billeted in pre-fabricated Nissen huts across the area.

The sky armada on Market Garden's D-Day was preceded by some 1,400 bombers to soften up the landing zones. Then came over 2,000 transport aircraft, including nearly 500 gliders, packed with equipment as well as men, pulled by tugs at the end of 300-foot tow ropes. Accompanying the whole were some 1,500 fighter planes to make sure the Luftwaffe couldn't interfere.

Since the 101st Airborne's zone was closest to Second Army's start-line near the Dutch border along the Maas-Escaut Canal, the bulk of the first day's heavy weapons- bearing gliders went to British 1st Airborne and the US 82nd, since they would need to self-sustain longer. The 101st would receive its full glider lift on D+1, bringing artillery, jeeps, and more troops.

The aircraft stream was divided into two routes, with the 1st Airborne and 82nd on the upper leg, coming in from the North Sea over Holland, and the 101st Airborne on a southern leg, crossing Belgium. By now the Germans had lost their radar stations in France so were unaware of the airborne invasion until it was upon them. Anti-aircraft fire opened up as the air fleets neared their objectives, causing some losses, but the landings as a whole were a success.

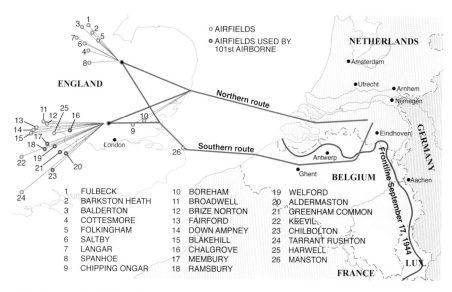

1	FULBECK	10	BOREHAM	19	WELFORD
2	BARKSTON HEATH	11	BROADWELL	20	ALDERMASTON
3	BALDERTON	12	BRIZE NORTON	21	GREENHAM COMMON
4	COTTESMORE	13	FAIRFORD	22	KEEVIL
5	FOLKINGHAM	14	DOWN AMPNEY	23	CHILBOLTON
6	SALTBY	15	BLAKEHILL	24	TARRANT RUSHTON
7	LANGAR	16	CHALGROVE	25	HARWELL
8	SPANHOE	17	MEMBURY	26	MANSTON
9	CHIPPING ONGAR	18	RAMSBURY		

AIRFIELDS
AIRFIELDS USED BY 101st AIRBORNE

Left:
101st Airborne's route to Holland and another rendezvous with destiny.

Below left:
Gen. Lewis H. Brereton, commanding First Allied Airborne Army, at Aldermaston. He's talking to Lt-Col. William B. Whitacre (second from right), CO of 434th Troop Carrier Group, and Col. Joseph Harper, CO of the 327th Glider Infantry Regiment, which will leave on D+1.

Bottom left:
Gen. Maxwell Taylor, the 101st AB Division's commanding officer, flew from Welford with 1st Bn 502nd PIR, whose CO, Lt-Col. Patrick Cassidy (second from right), is helping Maxwell don his chute.

Below:
Gen. Maxwell Taylor bids Welford farewell.

19

SEABORNE ECHELON

D+1 TO D+7   SEPT. 18 TO 24, 1944

	HQ. 101 A/B DIV.	HQ. CO. 101 A/B DIV.	M.P. PLAT., 101	327 GLI. INF.	501 PARA. INF.	502 PARA. INF.	506 PARA. INF.	HQ. BTRY. DIV. ARTY.	321 GLI. FA. BN.	377 PARA. FA. BN.	907 GLI. FA. BN.	81 A/B AA AT BN	326 A/B ENGR. BN	326 A/B MED CO.	426 A/B QM. CO.	801 A/B ORD CO.	101 A/B SIG CO.	101 A/B RECON. PLAT.	TOTALS
NO. OF PERSONNEL	17	38	3	118	94	(B)90	(A)90	27	(C)48	106	50	267	39	24	10	30	16	0	1077
2 1/2 TON TRUCKS	0	6	0	24	26	25	26	4	8	11	8	16	11	3	2	1	5	0	176
1 1/2 TON TRUCKS	0	0	0	1	1	1	1	0	1	0	1	1	1	1	0	0	0	0	9
3/4 TON TRUCKS	0	4	1	8	3	3	2	2	1	0	12	1	4	1	0	0	2	0	44
1/4 TON TRUCKS	7	2	2	5	0	0	2	2	2	15	2	18	0	0	0	14	0	0	71
1 TON TRAILERS	0	4	1	14	0	15	16	5	8	11	8	0	8	0	0	0	2	0	88
1/4 TON TRAILERS	5	1	1	5	0	0	0	1	0	0	0	18	0	0	0	14	0	0	45
BULLDOZERS	0	0	0	0	0	0	0	0	0	0	0	0	2	0	0	0	0	0	2

REMARKS

(A) 1 EN wounded
2 EN missing
Destroyed: 1 - 2½-ton truck
1 - 1-ton trailer
1 - ¾-ton truck

(B) 1-ton trailer wrecked enroute.

(C) 1 - 2½-ton truck had break down enroute later picked up by 801st AB Ordnance Company.

NOTE:
Sea echelon loaded on D + 1, sailed from Southampton on D + 2, arrived Omaha Beach on D + 3; first half left on morning of D + 3 and arrived Bourg Leopold evening of D + 4, arrived Division Service Area at Z on evening of D + 5; second half left on evening of D + 3, arrived Bourg Leopold evening of D + 5, arrived Division Service Area evening of D + 6.

Above and opposite, top:

From the official *Report of Airborne Phase Operation "Market,"* "The parachute echelon of the 101st Airborne Division consisted of 436 C-47 transport planes carrying some 6,809 parachutists of the Division. 424 planes dropped on D-Day, and 12 planes carrying Battery B, 377th Parachute Field Artillery Battalion, with 140 personnel and 6 guns, dropped on D+3... Jump casualties were less than 2% of the total number... A total of 988 CG4A Gliders took off from departure bases in the UK over a period of 7 days. 767 of these gliders landed without incident on the designated LZ. Approximately 5,000 men took off from the UK and some 4,800 eventually joined their units in the combat zone... The seaborne echelon of the Division consisted of 1,077 personnel and 444 vehicles of all types. This echelon loaded on D+1 and sailed from Southampton on D+2. It arrived at Omaha Beach on D+3, where it was divided into two serials. The first serial left the beach on the morning of D+3 and ... closed in the Division service area at ZON on the evening of D+5... The second serial closed in the Division service area on the evening of D+6.

Right:

Commander of 101st Airborne divisional artillery, Brig. Anthony C. McAuliffe, became assistant division commander when Don Pratt died on June 6, 1944. He is best remembered for the response "Nuts," to the suggestion that the encircled defenders of Bastogne should surrender. Here he's talking to Lt-Col. William B. Whitacre, 434th TC Group commander who would be McAuliffe's tug pilot.

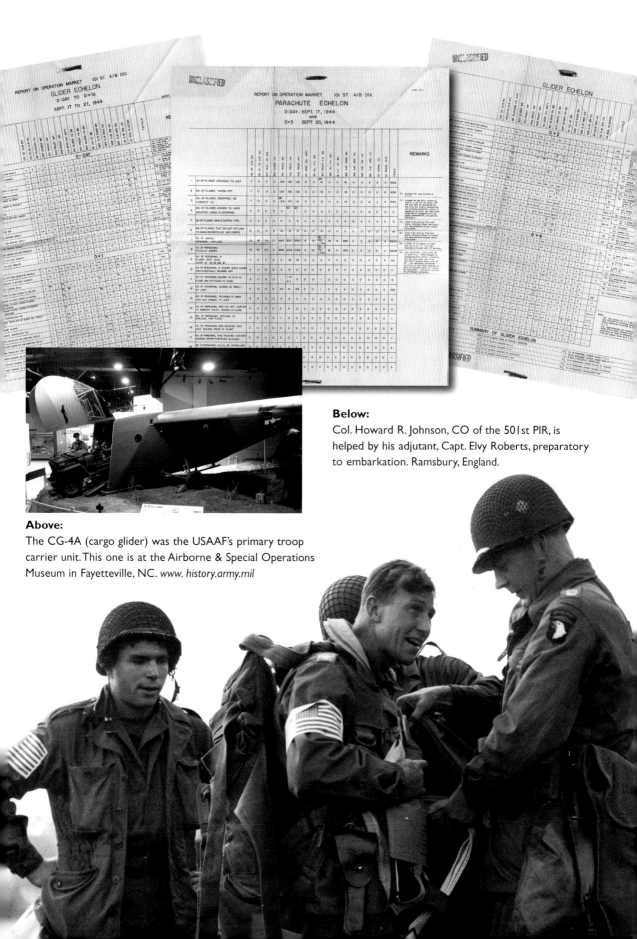

Above:
The CG-4A (cargo glider) was the USAAF's primary troop carrier unit. This one is at the Airborne & Special Operations Museum in Fayetteville, NC. *www. history.army.mil*

Below:
Col. Howard R. Johnson, CO of the 501st PIR, is helped by his adjutant, Capt. Elvy Roberts, preparatory to embarkation. Ramsbury, England.

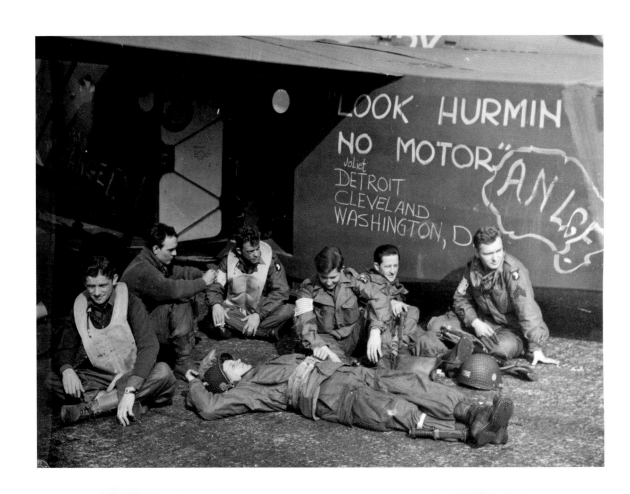

Opposite, above:
The glider lift on D+1 was postponed from morning till afternoon because of fog and all flights were switched to the southern route. The official report says, "The glider lift on D+2 was dispersed because of heavy fog encountered over the Channel and along the coast. Of some 384 gliders that took off on this date, only 209 landed safely on the designated LZ. Many others returned to the UK or landed on the continent." At Greenham Common, men of 377th FA Bn await their mission.

Opposite, below:
Brig-Gen. McAuliffe gives the secondwave crews and pilots a motivational speech.

Left:
The 1st Bn 501st PIR drops into Holland.

Below left:
Ft. Campbell-based BG Don F. Pratt Memorial Museum has nearby the historic C-47 Brass Hat (42-100828) that saw action towing gliders on D-Day (the 506th PIR from Upottery), in Operation "Dragoon," and Operation "Market," as well as being involved in supply drops to the garrison at Bastogne and, finally, Operation "Varsity." The Don F. Pratt Museum was established in 1956 as a division museum for the 101st Airborne Division.
Tom Timmermanns

Left:
The parachute echelon of the Division began its drop at 13:00 on D-Day. The 501st PR, with two platoons of 726th AEB attached, dropped on two DZs two miles west of Veghel and the other some three miles northwest. The 502nd PIR, with three platoons of 326th AEB attached, landed on DZ B without enemy opposition and all battalions were assembled by 15:00. The 506th PIR landed on DZ C without enemy opposition.

Below left:
Parachutes dot the area around Heeswijk Castle (at DZ A). Having landed, as soon as he could, Col. Harry Kinnard, CO 1st Bn 501st PIR, headed toward Veghel, leaving a small group of wounded and some guards behind. Compare the accuracy of this daytime drop with that of the 101st over Normandy in June!

Right, Main Photo:
1st Bn, 501st PIR, on its way. Leading the 45-aircraft formation is Col. Whitacre, the 434th Group commander. This photo was taken from the astrodome of his C-47.

Inset 1 and 2:
This pair of photos is officially dated the 23rd, but *After The Battle*—the yardstick for any researcher—suggests it is more likely to be the Skytrain of 1Lt. Jesse M. Harrison of the 435th Group which crashed on the 19th, during the second wave of drops.

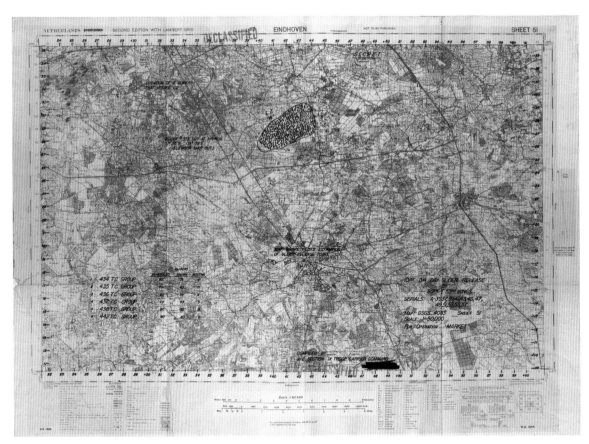

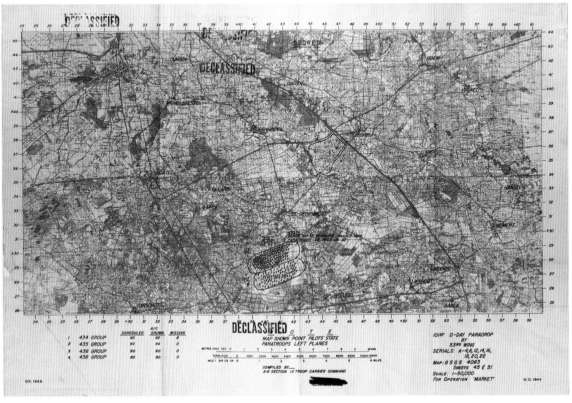

26

Opposite:
After the event IXth Troop Carrier Command identified where pilots stated that they dropped their loads. Dispersal was good and most troops were immediately ready for action.

Above:
There are always casualties, and airborne delivery is a dangerous occupation. The above photo shows the result of two gliders colliding in midair above their LZ. Men of 506th PIR rushed to help. *After the Battle*, as usual, has all the details of names and units.

Right:
The somber silhouette of a dead paratrooper caught up in telegraph wires.

Taking the Bridges

THE DAYTIME DROP was a relief to veterans of the 101st Airborne Division, who in Normandy had made their first combat jump in utter darkness, hardly any of them hitting their landing zones. That entire first night in Normandy had been chaos.

In Holland both the pilots and paratroopers could see what they were doing so could assemble quickly. Pathfinders marked the LZs in advance, and though one of the 101st's advance Pathfinder transports was shot down, even then the paratroopers needed only an hour or two to coalesce.

Achieving surprise in the German rear areas, the Screaming Eagles were quickly able to secure their bridges at the villages of St. Oedenrode and Veghel. But at the crucial one at Son, which spanned the Wilhelmina Canal, they encountered a German 88 firing straight down the highway. The 506th Parachute Infantry Regiment tried a flank attack, only to encounter two more 88's that ripped apart their assault. The Screaming Eagles persisted and valiantly fought through, knocking out the enemy guns and their supporting infantry, but when they were 50 yards away from the bridge the Germans suddenly blew it to smithereens. Now there was a problem.

The division's commander, Maxwell Taylor, had prepared for this contingency by ordering a company of the 502nd PIR to seize a back-up bridge at Best, four miles to the north. It was thought to be lightly defended; however, in one of the first nasty shocks of the campaign, there were 1,000 German troops there. Due to Allied neglect of the approaches to Antwerp, elements of German Fifteenth Army had escaped from the coast and had begun pouring south. The lone airborne company was decimated and its survivors pinned down short of the bridge.

Meanwhile Taylor had his engineers establish a footbridge over the canal at Son, and paratroopers crossed it single-file. But by then darkness had arrived; Eindhoven would have to wait for the morning.

Right:
The main events of D-Day, September 17, 1944. 1/501st PIR lands DZ A1. The rest of the 501st lands on DZ A. 502nd PIR lands on DZ B and 505th PIR on DZ C. Other elements of the division land by parachute and glider LZ W.

Below:
Troops move off the LZ. The jeep at right is one of 32 brought in by glider.

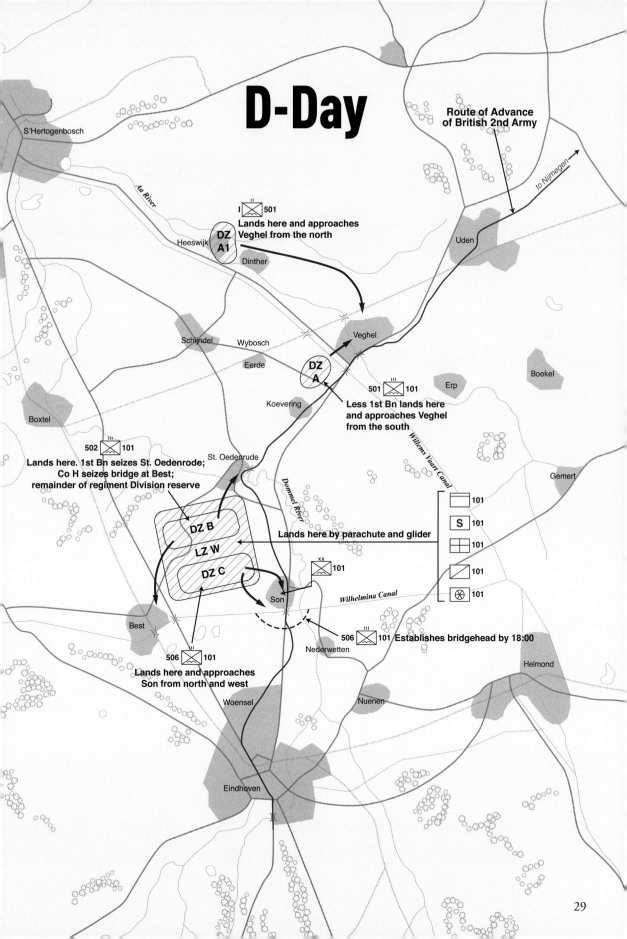

D-Day

Route of Advance of British 2nd Army

to Nijmegen

S'Hertogenbosch

Aa River

Heeswijk

Dinther

I ⊠ 501

Lands here and approaches Veghel from the north

DZ A1

Uden

Schijndel

Wybosch

Eerde

Veghel

DZ A

501 ⊠ 101

Erp

Boekel

Less 1st Bn lands here and approaches Veghel from the south

Koevering

Boxtel

502 ⊠ 101

Lands here. 1st Bn seizes St. Oedenrode; Co H seizes bridge at Best; remainder of regiment Division reserve

St. Oedenrode

Dommel River

Willems Vaart Canal

Gemert

	101
S	101
⊞	101
⧄	101
⊗	101

DZ B

LZ W

DZ C

Lands here by parachute and glider

xx ⊠ 101

Son

Wilhelmina Canal

Best

506 ⊠ 101

Lands here and approaches Son from north and west

Nederwetten

506 ⊠ 101 **Establishes bridgehead by 18:00**

Helmond

Woensel

Nuenen

Eindhoven

29

Above:
3rd Bn 501st PIR lands on DZ A, outside Eerde. Both pictures were taken at the crossroads of two rural dirt tracks, locally known as Wolven Steeg and Veerse Heide. *Battledetective.com*

Above:
Heeswijk-Dinther—men of 1st Bn 501st PIR move through School Straat near the house named "Hogenhof." This was the main road to Veghel. A new parallel road now runs behind these houses. The paras reached their objective within two hours. *Battledetective.com*

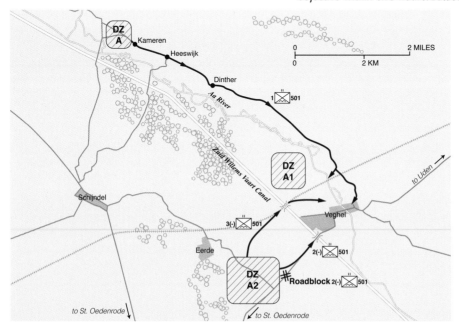

Left:
The capture of Veghel.

Opposite, top:
This doctor's house in Veghel acted as HQ for the 501st PIR. In its grounds (top right) is the 101st's Kangaroo monument.
Peter Anderson

Opposite, below left and right:
The Signal Corps Combat Assignment Team bag Fallschirmjäger prisoners on September 22. *Yank Reenactment*

Above:
Veghel's Airborne Monument harks back to the 101st Airborne's radio call sign—"Kangaroo."
Peter Anderson

Left:
The Liberation Chapel at Heeswijk-Dinther includes a small sculpture of an American paratrooper.
Havang(nl)/WikiCommons (CC0 1.0)

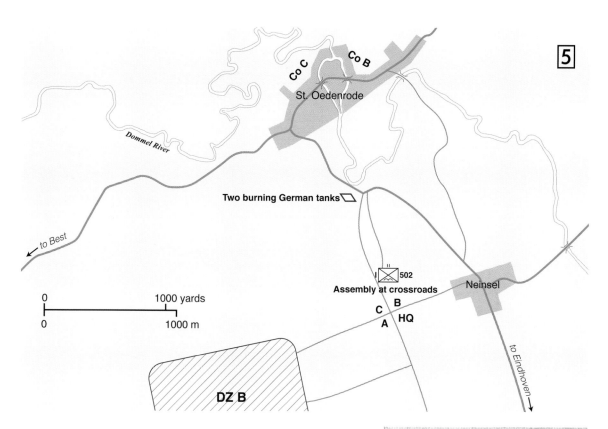

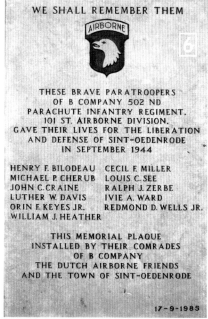

I and 2 Two plaques in the grounds of Heeswijk Castle: the first commemorates 501st PIR; the second, "Lt. Col. Francis Sampson, Chaplain, 101st US Airborne Division, parachuted here on September 17, 1944. Landing in the air on top of another parachutist, the two fell into the castle moat. Together they climbed out, but Father Sampson first had to dive again to recover his equipment. To remember this remarkable event this plaque was placed here in September the 17th, 1944. – Deceased 28th of January 1996."
Havang(nl)/WikiCommons (CC0 1.0)

3 "Monument for the Dutch" in St. Oedenrode: "Dedicated to the people of the Corridor by the veterans of the 101st Airborne Division, in grateful appreciation of their courage, compassion and friendship."
Richard Hermes/wikicommons (CC BY-SA 3.0 NL).

4 Heeswijk Castle was initially turned into an aid post for the wounded left behind after the drop, but it was soon retaken by the Germans and Heeswijk-Dinther stayed in the front line for some time.
Kasteelbeer/WikiCommons (CC BY-SA 3.0 NL)

5 The capture of St. Oedenrode by 1st Bn 501st PIR.

6 The former town hall in St. Oedenrode sports a plaque in memory of the men of B Co 502nd PIR who died fighting in the area.
Michielverbeek/Wiki Commons (CC BY-SA 4.0)

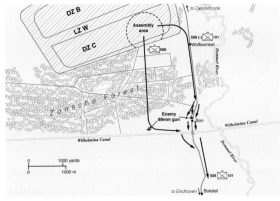

Above:
The Germans blew the bridge at Son in the faces of the 506th PIR.

Above right:
A memorial fountain at Son commemorates the 101st Division. *Peter Anderson*

Right:
The fight at Zonhove sanatorium was commemorated after the war by this memorial. *Peter Anderson*

Below:
Pvt. Bernard M. Takla, gives gum to a little Dutch girl.

Left:
This photo shows Catholic Chaplain (Capt.) Manus McGettigan nearest the camera and Protestant Chaplain (Capt.) Tildon S. McGee a few yards in front of him on DZ C. Both Chaplains belonged to the 506th PIR.

Center left:
"The Parachutist" at Son. The panel reads: "Liberated on September 17, 1944, by the 506th PIR and elements of the 326th Airborne Engineers. This town was the command post of the 101st Airborne Division during the first three days of the Holland campaign. The 506th Parachute Field Artillery, and the 81st Airborne AA Battalion, successfully repulsed all attacks on this position from D-Day to D+3 thereby enabling Div HQ to establish the command function so necessary to the success of the overall mission...."
Peter Anderson

Left:
Dutch civilians identify map locations for men of HQ 506th PIR, in front of the Merks Farm on the Son LZ.

1 In memory of Joe Mann, 502nd PIR, who won the Medal of Honor on September 9 at Best when a grenade "landed within a few feet.... Unable to raise his arms, which were bandaged to his body, he yelled 'grenade' and threw his body over the grenade." *Peter Anderson*

2 and 3 Plaque remembering Easy Company of 506th PIR— The Band of Brothers—on the facade of Paulushoef (3) in Son. *Alex P. Kok/WikiC (CC BYSA 3.0 NL)*

4 The Pelican monument to Joe Mann by Ard. Berntsen was placed on the road to Son in 1956. The pelican atop the concrete pillars is the oldest-known Christian symbol for total selfsacrifice. *Peter Anderson*

5 The fight for the bridge at Best. Most of 501st PIR dropped outside Veghel on DZ A and by 15:00 had already taken its four bridges, their initial objectives. 502nd PIR landed on DZ B and seized St. Oedenrode and its bridge over the Dommel. Part of the 3rd Bn attacked the road bridge at Best, but was forced away after a strong counterattack. 506th PIR landed on DZ C, but after fighting through to the main bridge over the Wilhelmina Canal at Son the Germans blew it up. This made the bridge at Best crucial and the battle to take it raged.

6 Liberation Route marker on the N620 in the woods between Best and Son.

7 The memorial to Lt-Col. Robert G. Cole who won the Medal of Honor at Carentan. He was killed in action here on September 18, and is buried at the American Cemetery in Margraten. *Both Peter Anderson*

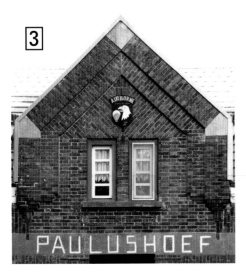

THE EAGLE WILL ALWAYS SCREAM FOR OUR FALLEN BROTHERS
MAY THE WORLD   NEVER FORGET

AIRBORNE

506TH P.I.R. 101ST AIRBORNE DIVISION
'E' COMPANY
OPERATION MARKET GARDEN 1944

PAULUSHOEF

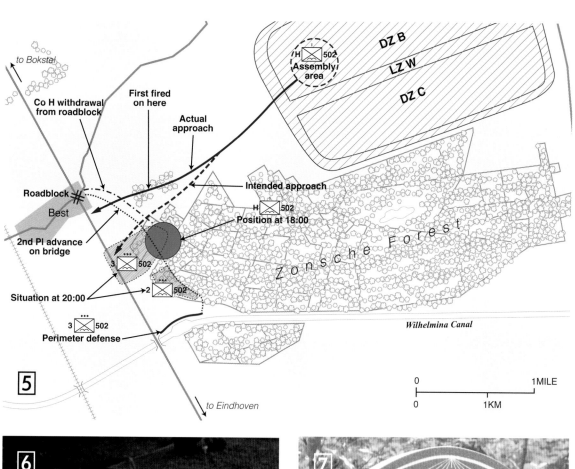

to Bokstel

Co H withdrawal
from roadblock

First fired
on here

Actual
approach

DZ B

LZ W

DZ C

H ⊠ 502
Assembly
area

Intended approach

Roadblock

Best

H ⊠ 502
Position at 18:00

2nd Pl advance
on bridge

3 ⊠ 502

Situation at 20:00

2 ⊠ 502

Z o n s c h e F o r e s t

Wilhelmina Canal

3 ⊠ 502
Perimeter defense

5

to Eindhoven

0   1MILE

0   1KM

6

7

LT. COL.
ROBERT G. COLE
MEDAL OF HONOR
18 SEPT. 1944
GESNEUVELD
VOOR ONS

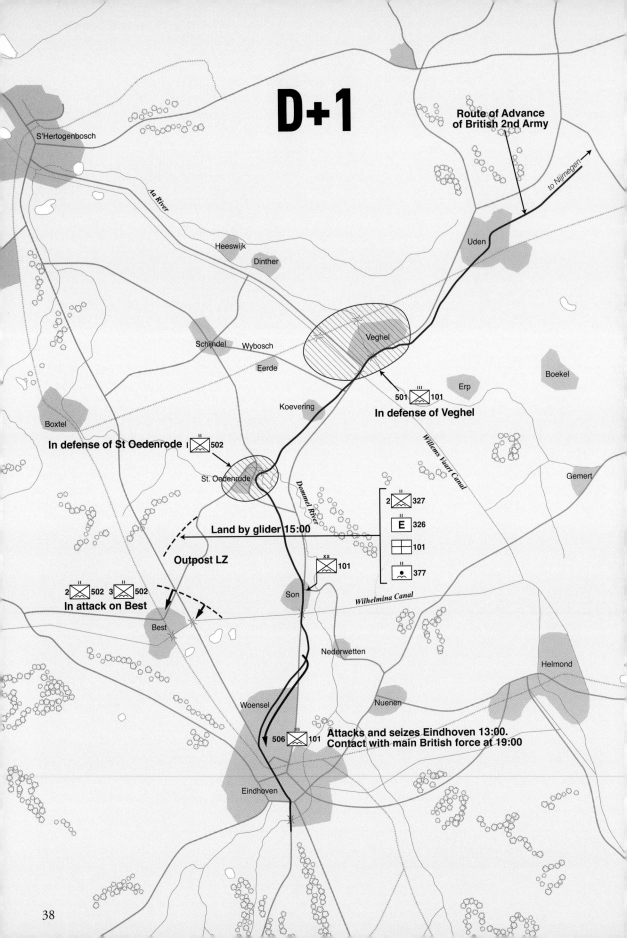

D+1

Route of Advance of British 2nd Army

to Nijmegen

S'Hertogenbosch

Aa River

Heeswijk

Dinther

Uden

Veghel

Schijndel   Wybosch

Eerde

Boekel

Koevering

501 ⊠ 101

In defense of Veghel

Erp

Willems Vaart Canal

In defense of St Oedenrode I ⊠ 502

Boxtel

St. Oedenrode

Dommel River

Gemert

2 ⊠ 327

E 326

⊞ 101

● 377

Land by glider 15:00

Outpost LZ

xx
⊠ 101

Son

2 ⊠ 502   3 ⊠ 502

In attack on Best

Best

Wilhelmina Canal

Nederwetten

Helmond

Woensel

Nuenen

506 ⊠ 101

Attacks and seizes Eindhoven 13:00. Contact with main British force at 19:00

Eindhoven

Opposite:
D+1 and still no artillery has arrived. The second lift is postponed to the afternoon because of fog.

Above:
The gliders of the second lift start arriving on LZ W at 14:00.

Left:
Another jeep is unloaded—vital to manage the extent of the 101st's operational area.

Below:
Paratroopers of the 506th PIR move east on Kerk Straat, Eindhoven. The next day this street would suffer extensive damage from a German bombing raid. It explains why the buildings' fronts on the left in the "now" photo have receded, creating a wider sidewalk. *Battledetective.com*

Taking Eindhoven

ON THE MORNING of D+1 the 506th PIR proceeded to the city of Eindhoven. The Germans had placed their main strength south of the town, opposite the Maas-Escaut Canal, to face the expected offensive from British Second Army. They had no reason to expect an attack from north of the town until the 101st Airborne suddenly appeared behind it.

Nevertheless, German units retreating from Son took up position, joined by ad hoc units who had been informed of the airborne incursion. Guns covered the highway, while a multitude of machinegun nests were in place. The Screaming Eagles' 1st Battalion/506th had taken heavy casualties at Son, so this time it was the 2nd and 3rd battalions that led the way.

After a brief flurry of combat they broke into the city—Holland's fifth largest—only to find their greatest opposition yet. Thousands upon thousands of Dutch civilians came pouring into the streets to celebrate their liberation. The paratroopers could hardly wade through the throng, and some had little wish to either as they were surrounded by happy civilians holding out cakes, fruit and wine, shaking hands with men, getting hugs by women, kissing babies and the rest.

Eindhoven, as a staging area for the Germans, was largely manned by rear-area supply or occupation troops, and Dutch civilians were helpful in pointing out their hiding places. The 101st, as a priority, took control of the city's four bridges over the Dommel River, and then systematically rounded up German soldiers.

By noon the city and its bridges had been seized, slightly behind schedule since it had been expected that XXX Corps would have arrived by then. But General Horrocks had been delayed also, encountering severe fireblocks along the highway, and his first

patrol only arrived at two o'clock on D+1. That evening the full British column began to pour in. Their first priority was to move up bridging equipment, and British engineers worked through the night to erect a Bailey Bridge at Son. Meantime the Germans had blown the bridge at Best, as two full battalions of the 502nd PIR were now fighting for that village. About mid-day the 101st's glider reinforcement arrived with little mishap, bringing not only part of the 327th Glider Regiment but light artillery and antitank guns. They would all be needed in the days that followed.

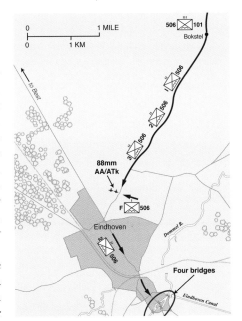

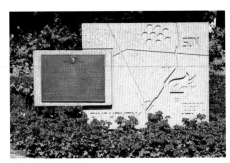

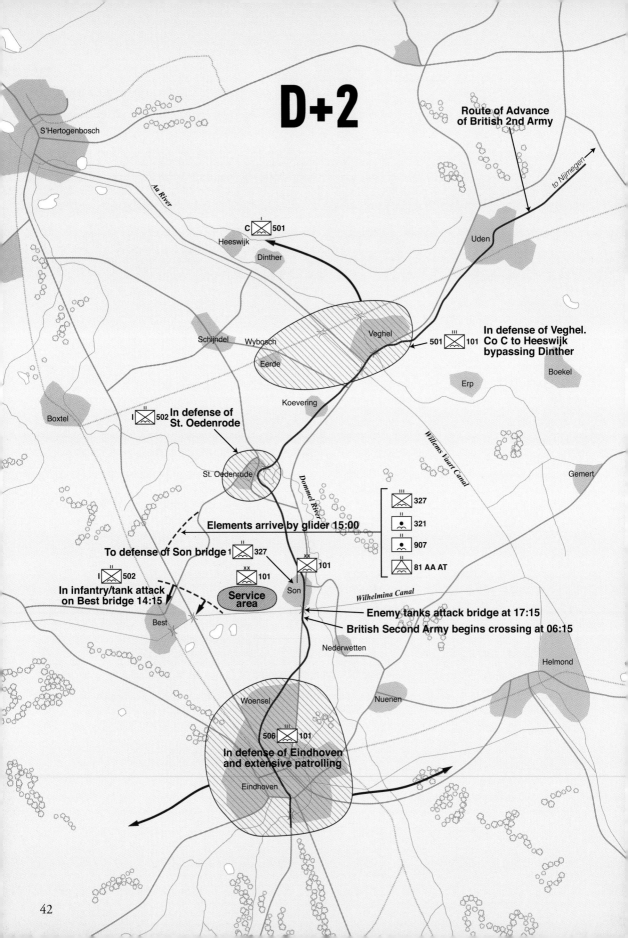

D+2

Route of Advance of British 2nd Army

to Nijmegen

Uden

S'Hertogenbosch

Aa River

C [ ] 501
Heeswijk

Dinther

501 [ ] 101
Veghel

In defense of Veghel. Co C to Heeswijk bypassing Dinther

Schijndel   Wybosch

Eerde

Boekel

Erp

Koevering

Boxtel

I [ ] 502 **In defense of St. Oedenrode**

St. Oedenrode

Dommel River

Williems Vaart Canal

Gemert

327
321
907
81 AA AT

Elements arrive by glider 15:00

To defense of Son bridge 1 [ ] 327

[ ] 502

101 Son

101 [ ]

In infantry/tank attack on Best bridge 14:15

Best

Service area

Wilhelmina Canal

Enemy tanks attack bridge at 17:15

British Second Army begins crossing at 06:15

Nederwetten

Helmond

Woensel

Nuenen

506 [ ] 101

In defense of Eindhoven and extensive patrolling

Eindhoven

Left:
On the 19th the 502nd PIR seized the crossing at Best, knocking out a number of 88s, killing 300, and taking over 1,000 captives.

Above:
14th Field Sqn, Royal Engineers, replaced the Son Bridge overnight on September 18/19 allowing the Grenadier Guards to rush toward Grave, 36 hours behind schedule.

Above right:
Shortly after crossing at Son the tanks reached Veghel where a bridge had been constructed by Capt. Thomas A. Norwood's A/326th Airborne Engineer Bn.
via D-Day Paratroopers Historical Center collection

Below:
The Son Bridge today. *Leo Marriott*

Left:

A Panther of 107th Panzer Brigade reached the Wilhelmina Canal near the repaired bridge at Son. It was knocked out by a 6pdr of 81st Anti-tank Bn rushed from the LZ. A second Panther was knocked out by a bazooka. Not realizing that the bridge itself was held by only a platoon (of A/506th) and engineers, the Germans withdrew. Paras examine the lead Panther's corpse, while the scene now is more placid.
Battledetective.com

Above right and right:

Men of the 506th PIR hitch a ride on a British Cromwell of A Sqn 15th/19th, The King's Royal Hussars in Eindhoven. This "fire brigade" force helped beat off German attacks in numerous locations (see Nuenen p.47).
Battledetective.com

Right:

A reconnaissance unit of 107th Panzer Brigade found this bridge on the outskirts of Eindhoven and judged it too weak to cross. Popular postwar belief has it that this bridge's weakness saved Eindhoven from a horrible tank battle. It is named after the gardener—Willem Hikspoors—who is said to have convinced the tank crew of this.
Battledetective.com

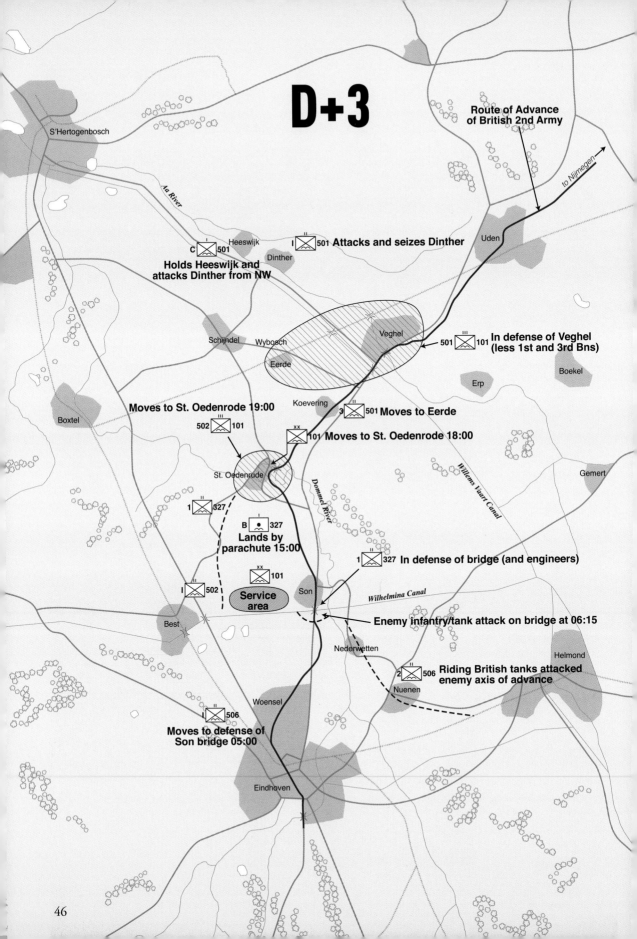

D+3

Route of Advance of British 2nd Army

to Nijmegen

S'Hertogenbosch

Aa River

Heeswijk

C ⊠ 501
Holds Heeswijk and attacks Dinther from NW

Dinther

I ⊠ 501 **Attacks and seizes Dinther**

Uden

Schijndel   Wybosch

Veghel

501 ⊠ 101 **In defense of Veghel (less 1st and 3rd Bns)**

Boekel

Eerde

Koevering

Erp

3 ⊠ 501 **Moves to Eerde**

Moves to St. Oedenrode 19:00

502 ⊠ 101

Boxtel

xx ⊠ 101 **Moves to St. Oedenrode 18:00**

Gemert

St. Oedenrode

Willems Vaart Canal

1 ⊠ 327

B ⊡ 327
Lands by parachute 15:00

Dommel River

1 ⊠ 327 **In defense of bridge (and engineers)**

xx ⊠ 101
Service area

Son

Wilhelmina Canal

I ⊠ 502

Best

Enemy infantry/tank attack on bridge at 06:15

Nederwetten

Helmond

2 ⊠ 506 **Riding British tanks attacked enemy axis of advance**

Nuenen

Woensel

I ⊠ 506
Moves to defense of Son bridge 05:00

Eindhoven

Opposite:
Having taken Eindhoven and made contact with XXX Corps, on September 19 the 101st Airborne's task was to keep the corridor open.

Above:
It did so in face of constant attacks, including—as we have seen—those by the newly arrived 107th Panzer Brigade around Son. Here a British XXX Corps truck explodes after being hit by a shell or mortar bomb on Hell's Highway. Movement along the Corridor stopped after this explosion, and trucks were stacked up on the road from Son to the Belgium border. Included were the boats needed for 82nd Airborne's crossing of the Waal at Nijmegen.

Above right:
At Nuenen a plaque commemorates the fallen of E Co 506th PIR: "The Eagle will always scream for our fallen brothers. May the world never forget 506th PIR 101st Airborne Division 'E' Company Operation Market Garden 17 September 1944." This is followed by the names of the fallen. On September 20, at Nuenen, E Co and British Cromwells of 15th/19th The King's Royal Hussars fought the 107th Panzer Brigade. The British lost two tanks and three men; four Americans were killed.
Alex P. Kok/WikiCommons (CC BY-SA 3.0)

Below:
In front of a 44th R T R Sherman, German Prisoners take a handcart to their compound in Son.

September 21 was a busy day. Amongst other duties, 1st Bn/501st PIR crossed the canal in the early morning at Heeswijk and patrolled during the day. 502nd PIR, with the 377th FA Bn attached, expanded its positions in the St. Oedenrode area. 2nd Bn 506th working with the 15/19 Hussars and 44th RTR, attacked the enemy at Nederwetten and forced them to withdraw.

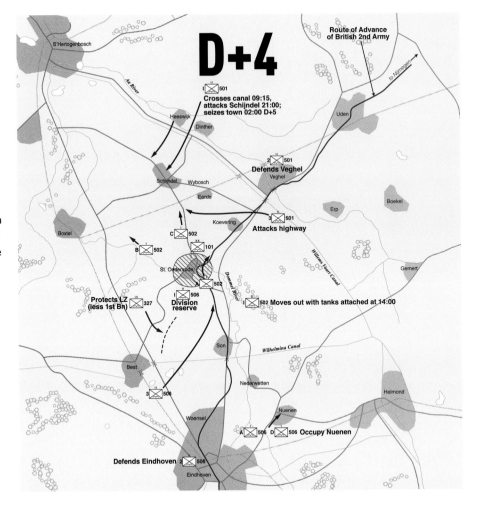

D+4

Route of Advance of British 2nd Army

to Nijmegen

S'Hertogenbosch

Aa River

Heeswijk

Dinther

Uden

1 501
Crosses canal 09:15, attacks Schijndel 21:00; seizes town 02:00 D+5

Schijndel Wybosch

2 501
Defends Veghel
Veghel

Eerde

Boekel

Erp

Koevering

3 501
Attacks highway

Boxtel

C 502

B 502

XX
101

Willems Vaart Canal

Gemert

St. Oedenrode

Dommel River

A 502

1 502 Moves out with tanks attached at 14:00

Protects LZ (less 1st Bn) 327

1 506
Division reserve

Son

Wilhelmina Canal

Best

3 506

Nederwetten

Helmond

Nuenen

Woensel

A 506 D 506 Occupy Nuenen

Defends Eindhoven 2 506

Eindhoven

Once British XXX Corps engineers had made it through Eindhoven and laid a bridge at Son, their schedule was 36 hours behind. But it didn't matter much, because the 82nd Airborne, though securing all their other objectives from the town of Grave on north, had been stymied at Nijmegen and its bridges across the wide Waal River. Elements of the 10th SS Panzer Division had arrived to contest its approaches. At the farthest Allied objective, Arnhem, British 1st Airborne had run into a buzzsaw of II SS Panzer Corps troops, though one battalion had managed to grasp a tenuous hold on the northern end of the city's highway bridge. Now it was D+2 in Market Garden, and German units throughout the Netherlands were being mobilized to resist what they now realized was a major Allied offensive. If Montgomery had expected a continuation of the Germans' headlong retreat out of France he was mistaken, as seasoned enemy units on both sides of the corridor counterattacked. From the north, more elements of German Fifteenth Army arrived, as did the Screaming Eagles' former antagonists, Fallschirmjäger Regiment 6. From the south, 107th Panzer Brigade emerged from the Reich. The Luftwaffe, too, was not idle, as over 100 bombers plastered the center of Eindhoven, where British vehicles were crammed up nose to fender. The carnage, both civilian and military, was immense. Assaults came in against the thin Allied

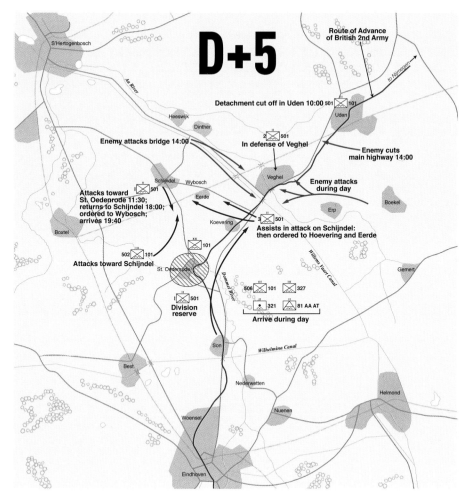

D+5

Route of Advance
of British 2nd Army

to Nijmegen

Detachment cut off in Uden 10:00 501 ⊠ 101
Uden

2 ⊠ 501
In defense of Veghel

Enemy attacks bridge 14:00

Enemy cuts
main highway 14:00

Veghel

Enemy attacks
during day

Attacks toward
St. Oedenrode 11:30;
returns to Schijndel 18:00;
ordered to Wybosch;
arrives 19:40

Schijndel Wybosch

Eerde

Boekel

Koevering

Erp

3 ⊠ 501
Assists in attack on Schijndel:
then ordered to Hoevering and Eerde

Boxtel

xx ⊠ 101

502 ⊠ 101

Attacks toward Schijndel

St. Oedenrode

Gemert

I ⊠ 501
Division
reserve

506 III 101   III 327

• 321   ▲ 81 AA AT

Arrive during day

Willems Vaart Canal

Dommel River

Son

Wilhelmina Canal

Best

Nederwetten

Helmond

Woensel

Nuenen

Eindhoven

S'Hertogenbosch

Aa River

Heeswijk

Dinther

corridor from both sides. Maxwell Taylor said it was like the old American West, "where small garrisons had to contend with sudden Indian attacks at any point." Indeed, while the 101st had to protect its highway, the Germans could assemble and stab from anywhere. Sometimes they cut across the highway, seizing crossroads, and the Screaming Eagles would have to counterattack to root them out. Then the Germans would stab again, cutting a different part. When they weren't achieving roadblocks on the highway, then mining it, they would execute fireblocks with tank or artillery fire, stopping all traffic. The 101st troopers had to protect both sides. Lead elements of XXX Corps had reached Nijmegen to assist 82nd Airborne, but on

D+6 Horrocks had to dispatch armor back south to help repel a German breakthrough near Veghel.

The problem had been partly anticipated in the Market Garden planning, which was why Second Army's XII Corps, on the left, and VIII Corps, to the right had advanced at the same time as XXX Corps. But beset with fierce resistance as well as terrible terrain, they could not keep up with Horrocks' spearhead formations. So for a 16-mile stretch, the practically naked flanks of "Hell's Highway" had to be primarily defended by the paratroopers, supported by elements of XXX Corps armor that could be spared from the main advance.

September 22 should have seen the 506th PIR move to Uden. Its advance guard had reached the village but then the Germans cut the road behind them. 107th Panzer Brigade, now enlarged into Kampfgruppe Walther, had moved from Son to Eerde overnight and attacked Veghel, pressing the 501st hard before being repulsed by British artillery. From the north, FJR6, German 59th Division, and other units, continued to stab at the corridor.

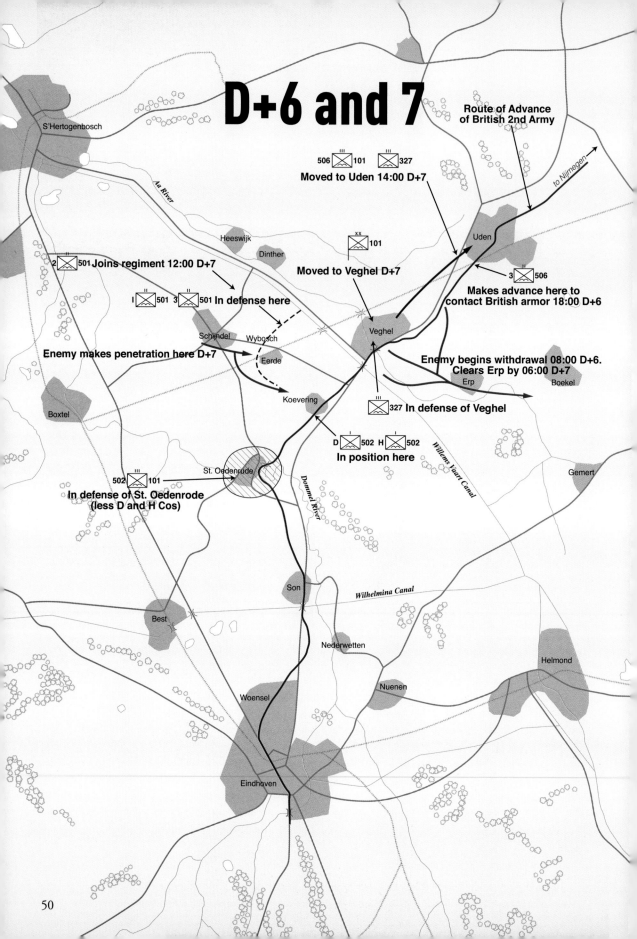

D+6 and 7

Route of Advance of British 2nd Army

506 [101] 327
Moved to Uden 14:00 D+7

to Nijmegen

101
Moved to Veghel D+7

2 [501] **Joins regiment 12:00 D+7**

Uden

3 [506]
Makes advance here to contact British armor 18:00 D+6

1 [501] 3 [501] **In defense here**

Schijndel   Wybosch

Enemy makes penetration here D+7

Eerde

Veghel

Enemy begins withdrawal 08:00 D+6. Clears Erp by 06:00 D+7

Erp   Boekel

Koevering

327 **In defense of Veghel**

D [502] H [502]
In position here

Willems Vaart Canal

Gemert

502 [101]
St. Oedenrode

In defense of St. Oedenrode (less D and H Cos)

Dommel River

Heeswijk
Dinther

Au River

S'Hertogenbosch

Boxtel

Son   Wilhelmina Canal

Best

Nederwetten

Helmond

Nuenen

Woensel

Eindhoven

50

Opposite:
The main events on September 23 and 24—501st's epic fight at Eerde; the German cutting of the highway at Koevering; and the relief of the units cut off at Udet by 32nd Guards Brigade from Grave.

Above and above left:
Soldiers of the 326th Airborne Engineers pass a burned-out GMC truck on Hoog Straat in Veghel. *Battledetective.com*

Left:
Remember all those practices in England? Here at the combat front a local tricycle is used as a transporter.

Right and below right:
On September 23 (D+6) the 107th Panzers attacked Veghel again, but the 101st's position was too strong for them. That afternoon—as is graphically described in *After the Battle*, vol 2—Shermans of C Sqn 44th RTR engaged the Panthers. This Firefly (above right) was knocked out as was a second Sherman, but not before it had dispatched this German command Panther (note extra aerials, right) killing at the same time Maj. Hans-Albrecht von Plüskow, CO of the battalion. A second Panther was knocked out by a cook of D/501st wielding a bazooka.

Below:
On September 24, D+7, 1st Bn, 501st PIR fought and won a bloody battle at Eerde, southwest of Veghel—the battle of the Sanddunes. Here they are showing some of their trophies.

The 101st met von der Heydte's FJR6 Fallschirmjäger again—this was the unit they had pushed out of Carentan—on September 24 at Eerde during the battle of the Sanddunes. The fighting was as tough as it had been in June, and as then the American paras came out on top. At the height of the battle a counterattack by 1st Bn drove off the defending Germans. This windmill (1, 2, and 6—seen postwar before rebuilding) is to the east of the battle area and was used as an OP, as was the church in the town (3 and 4). Both were shelled by the Germans for this reason. Postwar, in 1981, near the windmill, the Geronimo memorial to the 501st's victory (5) was unveiled. It and the windmill, which sports a number of related plaques, are the scene of a remembrance ceremony every September 17.

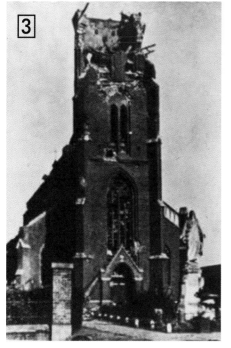

Photos: 1 MHB Verkuijlen/Wiki-Commons (CC BY-SA 3.0 NL); 4 Havang(nl)/WikiCommons (CC BY-SA 3.0); 5 Pimvantend/WikiCommons (CC BY-SA 3.0) 6 Heydra/Rijksdienst voor het Cultureel Erfgoed/WikiCommons (CC BY-SA 3.0 NL)

1 While 501st PIR fought at Eerde, the further German attack at Koevering succeeded and it took a concerted effort by 506th PIR attacking south and British forces attacking north to clear the road on the 25th, but only after it had been cut for 40 hours. British trucks from XXX Corps were shot up on the 24th and can be seen pushed into the ditch. They included 30 lorries from 536th Co, RASC, a number of which were carrying returning glider pilots of the 313th Troop Carrier Group, most of whom were lucky to escape.

2 This 44th Royal Tank Regiment Sherman was knocked out near Koevering on September 25 by a Jagdpanther. The Sherman was one of 10 supporting the 506th PIR.

3 The HQ of the 101st Airborne from D+4 onward was this "castle" at Henkenshage. *Richard Hermes/Wiki Commons (CC BY- SA 3.0 GB)*

4 The situation on September 25–27. The final battles on Hell's Highway—but by now the British 1st Airborne at Arnhem had been killed, captured, or their remnants withdrawn.

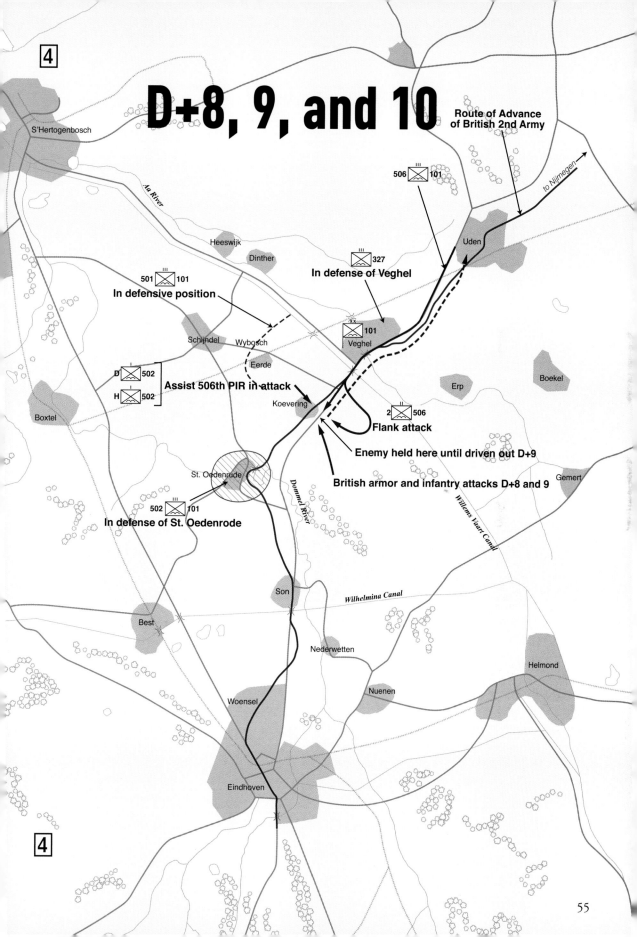

4

D+8, 9, and 10

Route of Advance of British 2nd Army

to Nijmegen

506 ||| 101

Uden

327

In defense of Veghel

501 ||| 101

In defensive position

Heeswijk

Dinther

Schijndel

Wybosch

XX
101
Veghel

Eerde

Boekel

Erp

D | 502

H | 502

Assist 506th PIR in attack

Koevering

2 || 506

Flank attack

Enemy held here until driven out D+9

Boxtel

St. Oedenrode

British armor and infantry attacks D+8 and 9

Gemert

502 ||| 101

In defense of St. Oedenrode

Dommel River

Willems Vaart Canal

Son

Wilhelmina Canal

Best

Nederwetten

Helmond

Nuenen

Woensel

Eindhoven

S'Hertogenbosch

Aa River

4

55

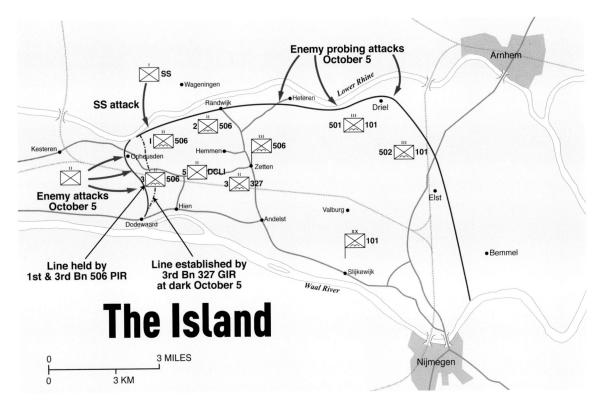

Enemy probing attacks
October 5

SS attack

Enemy attacks
October 5

Line held by
1st & 3rd Bn 506 PIR

Line established by
3rd Bn 327 GIR
at dark October 5

SS

Wageningen

Randwijk

Heteren

Lower Rhine

Driel

2 506

501 101

Kesteren

I 506

Hemmen

Opheusden

506

Zetten

502 101

5 DCLI

3 506

3 327

Hien

Elst

Dodewaard

Andelst

Valburg

101

Bemmel

Slijkewijk

Waal River

Nijmegen

The Island

0   3 MILES

0   3 KM

Above and
opposite, above:
The "Island" on
October 5 and 7.

Below:
A memorial to the
101st Airborne at
Heteren.
*Havang(nl)/WikiCommo
ns (CC BYSA 3.0)*

While the gallant fights of the U.S. paratroopers along Hell's Highway and at Nijmegen are part of the story of Market Garden, the most poignant part is the fate of British 1st Airborne, dropped at the farthest end of the string, across the Lower Rhine. Assured that armored and other support would reach them in two days, instead the paras became surrounded by two SS Panzer divisions and were nearly wiped out, despite the belated arrival of the Polish Brigade, whose airdrops had been delayed by weather.

Every fight the US 101st Airborne waged along Hell's Highway was to keep the road open for Allied strength to reach their compatriots in Arnhem. When the few remnants of 1st Airborne were brought back across the Rhine, on D+8, Operation Market Garden ended.

The fighting continued, however. Though the Allies had failed to seize their ultimate objective, they still owned a 55-mile salient into Holland with enemy troops on three sides. Now that VIII and XIIth Corps had moved up on the flanks,

the 101st was moved north to defend the vulnerable area between Nijmegen and Arnhem. Surrounded by the Waal and Lower Rhine rivers it was termed "the Island."

Here, throughout October and most of November, the 101st remained, beating off constant German probes while launching ones of their own. It was poor, exposed terrain where the mortar or machine-gun were king, even as both sides were plastered by the other's artillery. Gradually it became a strategic backwater as the Germans moved their best units south to contest US First Army's offensive against the Westwall and Third Army's bludgeoning attacks toward the Saar—even as they secretly built up major forces in reserve.

After 72 days of combat in Holland, the 101st Airborne was finally pulled out of the line and sent to Mourmelon, France to rest and recoup its losses. The paratroopers would have less than a month, however, before they would be called upon to repel another German thrust—this time the largest of them all—at the Battle of the Bulge.

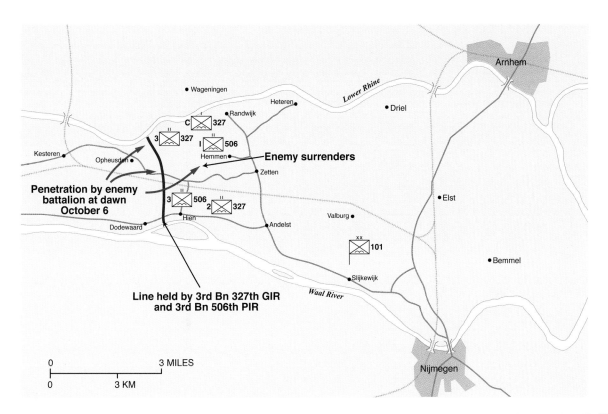

Map labels:
Arnhem
Wageningen
Heteren
Lower Rhine
Driel
Randwijk
C 327
3 327
I 506
Hemmen
Enemy surrenders
Kesteren
Opheusden
Zetten
Elst
Penetration by enemy
battalion at dawn
October 6
3 506
2 327
Hien
Valburg
Dodewaard
Andelst
xx 101
Line held by 3rd Bn 327th GIR
and 3rd Bn 506th PIR
Bemmel
Slijkewijk
Waal River
Nijmegen

0   3 MILES
0   3 KM

Below left:
Paras from 2/506th PIR between Opheusden and Randwijk.

Below right:
501st PIR on the Island. Here men of 3rd Pl, F/501st man an
MG position west of Heteren.
via D-Day Paratroopers Historical Center collection

Right, top:
The "Incredible Patrol" took place on October 29 at the behest of Gen. Higgins, who needed information on enemy dispositions north of the Rhine. Six men in total—Lt. Hugo Sims, a German speaking interrogator, and four from the I&R Pl, 501st PIR—crossed the river and landed east of Renkum. They slipped through enemy lines and reached the highway leading from Ede to Arnhem, hiding during the day in a house near the Ginkelse Heide. The next night the patrol captured 32 enemy officers and men, and took them back across the Rhine to the American HQ for interrogation.

Right, middle:
326th AB Medical Co ambulances hit by enemy bombs near Nijmegen, October 29. The company suffered three killed.

Right, below:
B/326th Engr Bn patroled and fought as infantry on the Island, here passing a PzKpfw II knocked out by artillery.
via D-Day Paratroopers Historical Center collection

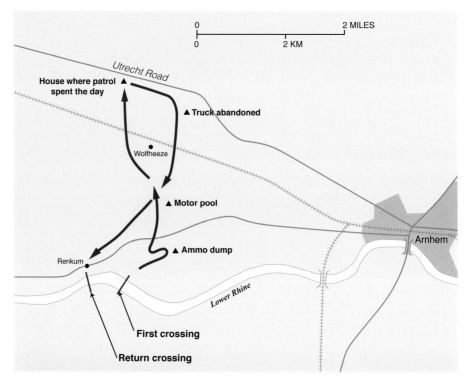

0 ____ 2 MILES
0 ____ 2 KM

Utrecht Road

▲ House where patrol spent the day

▲ Truck abandoned

● Wolfheeze

▲ Motor pool

● Renkum

▲ Ammo dump

Arnhem

Lower Rhine

First crossing

Return crossing

58

Off the Line

Left:
Heading for some R&R. After 72 days of combat, the 101st Airborne, at the end of November 1944, were the last US combat troops relieved from Market Garden. The division's rear detachment, including a medical unit of an officer and three men, stayed in Nijmegen until the group finally traveled to Camp Mourmelon in France, arriving December 1, 1944.

Below:
On November 25, at Weurt, the last men of the division embark on British trucks for Camp Mourmelon.

The Air Dimension

Left:
As well as initially dropping paratroopers and gliders, much of the further resupply of ground forces was by air. *The Report of Airborne Phase* identifies: "Percentage of recovery of resupply for entire operation. Glider resupply—95.9%. Resupply—41.4%" Beginning September 18, Eighth Air Force bombers were used. Here, a B-24 is seen over Son. Hit by flak after this low-level supply drop mission, the Liberator crashed near Udenhout with only one survivor.

Below left:
While ferocious fighting took place on the ground, the skies above Holland were also a battlefield. Here is shown a Spitfire IX of No. 441 (Canadian) Sqn which crashed SW of Nijmegen.

Below:
This monument commemorating the IXth Troop Carrier Command during Operation "Market Garden" is at Son. *Alex P. Cook/WikiCommons (CC BYSA 3.0)*

Left:
This 306th Squadron
Skytrain, having dropped
elements of the 506th PIR
as reinforcement, was
shot down and crashed
into a Jagdpanther of
schwere Panzer-Jäger
Abteilung 559 that had
been knocked out the
week before.

Below:
The "Wings of
Liberation" museum in
Best has this C-47 and a
Waco C-4A.
Tom Timmermans

Cemeteries

Below:
101st Airborne casualties were mainly taken to Zonhove Hospital in the center of Son. Those who died were placed in a temporary cemetery in the fields on the northern side of Son near Waterhoef farm. Later these remains went back to the US or to Margraten, depending on family wishes.

Right:
A monument remembering the US military cemetery in Son.
Wammes Waggel/WikiCommons (CC BY-SA 3.0)

Opposite, above:
Another temporary US cemetery, at Molenhoek, was just south of Nijmegen.

Opposite, below:
The Netherlands American Cemetery and Memorial at Margraten is the last resting place for many of 101st Airborne's Market Garden heroes. *Leo Marriott*

Bibliography

Bennett, David: *A Magnificent Disaster*; Casemate, 2008.

Bentley, Stewart W.: "The Dutch Resistance During Operation Market Garden"; www.pegasusarchive.org.

Cholewczynski, George F.: *Poles Apart*; Sarpedon, 1993.

Dear, I.C.B. and M.R.D. Foot (eds.): *The Oxford Companion to World War II*; Oxford University Press, 1995.

Griesser, Volker: *The Lions of Carentan*; Casemate, 2013.

Hendrikx, Peter, and De Trez, Michel: *Orange is the Color of the Day: Pictorial History of the 101st Airborne Division During the Liberation of Holland*; D-Day Paratroopers Historical Center Publishing, 2012.

Holt, Major and Mrs.: *Operation Market Garden*; Pen & Sword, 2012.

Kershaw, Robert: *It Never Snows in September*; Crowood Press, 1990.

Koskimaki, George: *Hell's Highway*; Presidio Press, 1989.

MacDonald, Charles B.: *US Army in WW2: ETO The Siegfried Line Campaign*; DoA, Washington DC, 1963.

Margry, Karel: *Operation Market Garden Then and Now* (two vols); After the Battle, 2002.

Miller, Victor. *Nothing Is Impossible*; Spellmount, 1994.

Operation Market Garden: ww2.marketgarden.com

Poyster, T. and B. Brown: *Fighting Fox Company*; Casemate, 2013.

Rapport, L. and Northwood, A.: *Rendezvous with Destiny*; 101st AB Assn, 1948.

Ryan, Cornelius: *A Bridge Too Far*; Simon & Schuster, 1974.

The 101st Airborne during World War II: ww2-airborne.us/18corps/101abn/101_statistics.html.

XVIII Corps: *Report of Airborne Phase Operation "Market"*; February 1945.

326th Airborne Medical Company information (see pp58–59) from WWII US Medical Research Centre website.

Van Lunteren, Frank: *The Battle of the Bridges*; Casemate, 2014.

Whitlock, Flint: *If Chaos Reigns*; Casemate, 2011.

Womer, J. and S. DeVito. *Fighting with the Filthy Thirteen*; Casemate, 2012.

Wood, W. Raymond: *Or Go Down in Flame*; Sarpedon, 1993.

www.Battledetective.com: various articles.

Key to Map Symbols

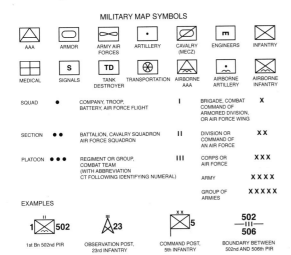

MILITARY MAP SYMBOLS

AAA	ARMOR	ARMY AIR FORCES
ARTILLERY	CAVALRY (MECZ)	ENGINEERS
INFANTRY	MEDICAL	SIGNALS
TANK DESTROYER	TRANSPORTATION	AIRBORNE AAA
AIRBORNE ARTILLERY	AIRBORNE INFANTRY	

SQUAD	•
SECTION	• •
PLATOON	• • •

COMPANY, TROOP, BATTERY, AIR FORCE FLIGHT	I
BATTALION, CAVALRY SQUADRON AIR FORCE SQUADRON	II
REGIMENT OR GROUP, COMBAT TEAM (WITH ABBREVIATION CT FOLLOWING IDENTIFYING NUMERAL)	III

BRIGADE, COMBAT COMMAND OF ARMORED DIVISION, OR AIR FORCE WING	X
DIVISION OR COMMAND OF AN AIR FORCE	XX
CORPS OR AIR FORCE	XXX
ARMY	XXXX
GROUP OF ARMIES	XXXXX

EXAMPLES

1⊠502 — 1st Bn 502nd PIR

△23 — OBSERVATION POST, 23rd INFANTRY

⊠5 — COMMAND POST, 5th INFANTRY

502 / 506 — BOUNDARY BETWEEN 502nd AND 506th PIR